# D'Nealian™ Handwriting

Author: Donald N. Thurber
Principal
Gibraltar Schools
Rockwood, Michigan

Adviser: Dale R. Jordan
Director of Diagnosis
Jordan-Adams Learning Center
Oklahoma City, Oklahoma

Scott, Foresman and Company
Editorial Offices: Glenview, Illinois

Regional Sales Offices: Palo Alto, California •
Tucker, Georgia • Glenview, Illinois •
Oakland, New Jersey • Dallas, Texas

# Contents

ISBN: 0-673-11530-5

Copyright © 1978,
Scott, Foresman and Company, Glenview, Illinois.
All Rights Reserved.
Printed in the United States of America.

2345678910-WEB-8584838281807978

# Materials

Softbound pupil text

Teacher's Edition

Duplicating Masters
(Manuscript)

Alphabet Cards

# Program Highlights

## Continuous skill progression

- The form of most lower-case manuscript letters is the basic form of the corresponding cursive letters.
- Simple joining strokes convert the lower-case manuscript alphabet to cursive.
- A continuous-stroke alphabet helps children develop a rhythm early in their handwriting experience.
- Writing lines, from the beginning, are close to adult size.
- Writing is slanted from the beginning.

## Focus on legibility

- Legibility, not machine-like perfection, is stressed.
- Individuality is accepted within the bounds of legibility.
- Appropriate adjustments in size are taught for different purposes.
- Applications of manuscript and cursive writing, according to legibility needs, are emphasized.

## Complete skill program

- Readiness games and exercises prepare children for handwriting.
- Complete letters—not component parts—are taught.
- Appropriate size variations are taught.
- Alignment and spacing are emphasized in writing without lines.
- Letters are joined in cursive as soon as they are taught.
- Print-awareness is systematically taught in Book 1.
- Uses for capitalization and punctuation are taught as letters and punctuation marks are presented.

## Real-life handwriting applications

- Career-awareness related to handwriting appears in books 3 through 8.
- Checks, journals, sales slips, charts, letters, notes, invitations, lists, and messages are presented for handwriting practice.
- Size variations—essential for filling out forms and applications—are systematically taught.
- Practice in writing without lines is included beginning at Book 1.

## Built-in assessment, review, and evaluation

- An assessment-and-review section appears at the beginning of every book, from grade 1 through grade 8.
- Review and evaluation lessons appear in every teacher's edition.

## Relationship reinforced between handwriting and school content areas

- Print awareness—a unique feature of Book 1—reinforces the relationship between reading and handwriting.
- Spelling, affixes, capitalization, and punctuation activities reinforce skills for language arts.
- Numbers and mathematical uses of handwriting are taught.
- Classifying, observing, and labeling exercises, important for science, are included.
- Map use reinforces social studies skills.
- Health and nutrition are emphasized.
- Reference sources—encyclopedias, dictionaries, thesauri, and the like—are used in handwriting lessons.

## Success oriented

- Letters are grouped for teaching by similarity of stroke.
- Handwriting skills are applied as soon as they are taught.
- Plenty of practice is provided.
- Letter models are presented for both left- and right-handed children.

## Thorough and easy-to-use Teacher's Edition

- Four-part teaching sections are easy to follow
- Objectives are clearly stated for each lesson.
- Teaching for a pupil-book page surrounds a full-color reduction of that page in the teacher's edition.
- Activities provide extra fun and practice related to handwriting lessons.
- Special Populations sections give hints for helping children with handwriting problems.

## Learner verification

- The D'Nealian method has been in use in classrooms for as long as ten years.
- Lessons are classroom tested.

## Visual appeal

- Colorful and varied styles of art and photography make the books appealing to children.
- Type is easy to read.

# About Handwriting

In spite of advances in modern communication machinery—television, citizen-band radios, computerized typewriters, teleprinters, and so on—handwriting is still an essential skill for today's functioning adult. Most people—be they clerks, lawyers, hairdressers, machinists, or scientists—have to write, sign, or compute something almost every day, as they go about the business of living and making a living.

And yet, think of the problems many adults encounter with handwriting. Many shrink from any display of their handwriting because it is illegible and unattractive. Others are embarrassed when they find their poor handwriting has led to errors in orders or in mail delivery. Still others are angry when they are judged as being sloppy or poor thinkers because the ideas they express in handwriting are impossible to read.

When and how does this widespread problem begin. Do children come to school with an aversion to writing? Evidence proves quite the contrary. Most children enter school eager and ready to learn to write; some have even taught themselves to write their own names or have teased the grown-ups in their families into teaching them well before they start school. What happens, then, that dulls so many children's interest in mastering a much anticipated skill?

It would seem that for many children, the traditional steps in teaching handwriting—first the circle-and-straight-line manuscript letter forms and then the arduous transition to the flowing, rhythmic, connected cursive letter forms—are more than they can cope with. The transition from manuscript to cursive, with the latter's often rigidly perfectionist models, which few children—or adults, for that matter—can emulate, pose particularly severe and long-lasting problems for many learners.

Since the problem is so widespread and frustrating, there has been a tendency to cast blame on children—for not trying hard enough (remember that lump on the second finger of *your* writing hand?)—or on teachers for not teaching properly or providing enough practice. Not much consideration has been given, however, to the possibility that there might be something amiss with the handwriting systems themselves—until now.

Scott, Foresman's *D'Nealian™ Handwriting* is the first new handwriting system developed in the past 50 years. It is a classroom teacher's answer to years of struggle and frustration—mixed with sympathy for student despair—in teaching handwriting the traditional way. After over 10 years of successful use in a number of classrooms, *D'Nealian™ Handwriting* has been developed into a K through 8 program that will make handwriting instruction a pleasant experience for student and teacher alike.

# About D'Nealian™ Handwriting

## Continuous skill progression

Scott, Foresman D'Nealian™ Handwriting is a simplified method of teaching handwriting. It solves many of the problems once thought to be inherent in teaching—and learning—beginning handwriting. It replaces the discontinuous skill progression with a logical program of *continuous skill progression.* From the very beginning of their handwriting instruction, children learn the basic letter forms, size, slant, rhythm, and spacing they will need for the writing they will do for a lifetime.

The D'Nealian method boosts early motivation by helping children write early and in an adult-like alphabet. Because children do not need to first learn individual component parts (circles, straight lines, and slant lines) and then to learn to join these parts into letters, they can start actual writing almost immediately. In *D'Nealian™ Handwriting,* Book 1, children write words as soon as they learn two letters, *a* and *d.* Children beginning D'Nealian manuscript writing have the thrill of knowing they are writing an alphabet that is similar to that used by the adults or older brothers and sisters in their families.

D'Nealian™ Manuscript

D'Nealian™ Cursive

*Letter forms.* The forms of most D'Nealian lower-case manuscript letters are the basic forms of the corresponding cursive letters. Each letter is made with a continuous stroke, except the dotted letters *i* and *j* and the crossed letters *f*, *t*, and *x*.

Because most letters are made with a continuous stroke, a beginning writer only needs to find the place on the paper once for each letter. This contrasts with from two to four pencil lifts for most letters made with circles and straight or slanted lines.

The transition from lower-case D'Nealian manuscript to cursive is so easy that it comes naturally to many children. With the exception of *f, r, s, v,* and *z,* manuscript letters become cursive letters with the addition of simple joining strokes. The most important of these strokes are the simple uphill stroke and the overhill stroke.

uphill stroke        overhill stroke

Even first-grade teachers will find highly motivated pupils trying to make the transition to cursive—the way "big people" write—on their own. The flowing rhythm of D'Nealian manuscript leads naturally to D'Nealian cursive.

The D'Nealian Program further simplifies writing by using the same numbers and punctuation in both manuscript and cursive.

*My name is Tami*
*I am in first grade*
*at Darrow School.*
*My teacher is Mrs.*
*Henderson.*

tall letters

*b d f h k l t* ----- and all capital letters ---

small letters

*a c e i m n o r s u v w x z*

descender letters

*g j p q y*

Slant. *D'Nealian™ Handwriting* teaches children to slant their letters from the beginning. If a child can be taught vertical alignment (most common with the circle-and-straight-line alphabets), he or she can just as easily be taught a slanted alignment. By slanting letters from the beginning, children benefit from another aspect of D'Nealian's continuous skill progression: they do not have to learn a new alignment for the transition to cursive.

Size. A third aspect of the D'Nealian program that contributes to continuity in skill progression is size. With very few exceptions, beginning writers meet with success when they start writing on one-half-inch ruled paper with a dotted midline (usually referred to as "third-grade" writing paper).* Children learning D'Nealian use one-half-inch ruled paper from kindergarten through third grade. For the first three or four years of learning handwriting—both manuscript and cursive—children do not have to adjust in several steps to narrower and narrower writing lines.

*Many teachers have long believed that even very young children do not need oversized writing lines. Controlled research is now appearing to support this belief. See "Special Paper for Beginning Handwriting: An Unjustified Practice?" by Glennelle Halpin and Gerald Halpin, *The Journal of Educational Research,* March 1976, Vol. 69, No. 7, pp. 267–269.

At fourth grade, D'Nealian recommends a change to standard ruled notebook paper (about two picas or one-third inch). This size is a typical adult size for writing and is used in the D'Nealian program from fourth through eighth grades.

Teaching—and learning—of size also has been simplified. In D'Nealian manuscript, there are only three heights for letters: tall, small, and letters with descenders. Letters either fill the entire line (from top line to bottom line), half a line (from middle line to bottom line), or have a descender (half a line below the bottom line).

The letters *t* and *d* are full tall letters. They do not fall short of the top line. This eliminates two "exceptions" in teaching and learning letters.

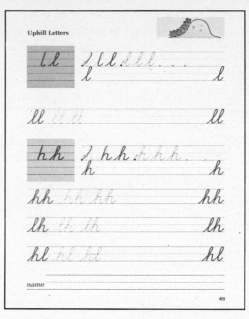

*Spacing.* Another aspect of D'Nealian that simplifies teaching handwriting is the way spacing is handled. Spacing is taught from the very beginning in both manuscript and cursive. As soon as children learn two letters in manuscript (*a* and *d*), they put the letters into words (*add* and *dad*). Thus, they are taught proper word spacing right from the beginning. When pupils have had four letters (*a*, *d*, *o*, and *g*), they write phrases (*a dog* and *a good dog*), moving smoothly into correct word spacing.

When the transition to cursive is made, D'Nealian also introduces proper spacing as early as possible. The first cursive letter taught is the letter *l*. When pupils have practiced the letter by itself, they immediately practice joining one *l* with another *l*. As children learn the next three cursive letters, they join each letter with others they have learned. By the time pupils learn their fifth and sixth letters, they write words. From the beginning of their cursive writing, children establish the rhythm of writing by joining letters. The skill of joining is not delayed until a large number of individual letters are learned.

*Rhythm.* Rhythm is an essential ingredient for effortless handwriting. The simple letter forms of the D'Nealian lower-case manuscript alphabet help children establish the essential rhythm from the beginning.

Each D'Nealian lower-case manuscript letter is made with a continuous stroke, except for crossing the *f*, *t*, and *x*, and dotting the *i* and *j*. Young children are not faced with the problem of trying to establish rhythm with an alphabet that requires joining component parts of letters. As a result, they establish a smooth, rhythmic flow in their handwriting from the beginning.

The transition to cursive comes naturally to children who begin writing with the D'Nealian method. Because they already have the basic rhythm of letter formation, children do little more than connect letters they know to form cursive letters.

## Flexible evaluation of handwriting

D'Nealian gives teachers and children flexibility in dealing with individual differences in handwriting. By its nature, handwriting is one of the most individual skills a person will learn. A person's handwriting is so distinctive that it is one of the three major characteristics—voiceprints, fingerprints, and handwriting—that law-enforcement agencies can use to identify that individual.

Since handwriting develops into such a mark of individuality, it is fruitless for teachers and children to spend endless hours trying to emulate a machine-perfect handwriting model. A child's self-image can suffer when his or her handwriting—however legible—is criticized for minor deviations from a perfect model. How much more encouraging for children to be praised for fine efforts within a wider range of legibility.

Legibility is the key to "correctness" in D'Nealian Handwriting. Minimum standards in form, size, and slant allow flexibility for individual differences.

Legibility in the form of letters means that certain basic criteria for letter form must be met. In the letter a, for example, the round part of the letter must be open, the letter must close at the top, and the ending stroke should align with the bottom of the letter.

These a's are acceptable in the D'Nealian handwriting program:

*a a a a a*

These a's are not acceptable:

*u d o a*

Similar variations may be made in other letters without losing legibility.

D'Nealian manuscript letters are presented with a slight right-hand slant. Some children, however, will not naturally use a right-hand slant. They may print vertically or with a slight left-hand (or backhand) slant. As long as the slant is consistent for all letters and not so extreme that it interferes with legibility, it is acceptable.

These slants are acceptable.

*grandmother*
*grandmother*
*grandmother*

These slants are not acceptable.

*grandmother*

The D'Nealian program also allows flexibility in size. Although one-half-inch and one-third-inch writing lines are presented in models, reasonable sizes are acceptable. Again, the key is legibility, as well as practicality. A very large size becomes impractical for a writer who has a lot to say. A very small size may lose legibility and put a burden on the reader.

However, within a range of practicality and legibility, D'Nealian accepts different sizes.

*Septe*

*I am in first*

*Today is Thur*

In D'Nealian books, children see examples of "real" handwriting in different sizes. At higher levels, children are given specific practice in keeping their letters in the correct proportion. For example, pupils are reminded that a tall letter, such as *l*, should be twice the height of a small letter, such as *e* or *i*. The proportion is generally more important than the size.

# Lesson organization

The teaching for Book 1 is divided into thirty sections with four lessons in each section. It is suggested that one section be used for a week's work. This allows specific teaching lessons on four days with a free day for other applications on the fifth day.

**Section number** and lesson content give a brief overview of the section.

**Objectives** are clearly stated for each lesson.

**Teaching** gives specific suggestions for teaching from a page in the pupil's book or for providing preparation, review, or evaluation.

**Oral directions** are provided when letters are first taught. The first part of the directions is a detailed description of letter strokes. The second part is a shortened form that can be used as a reminder after initial instruction.

## Lesson 1

### SECTION 19
Pages 68, 69, 70

**Lesson 1, page 68**
**Lesson 2, page 69**
**Lesson 3, page 70**
**Lesson 4, review**

### Lesson 1, page 68

**Objectives**
• Traces and writes manuscript letter A.
• Writes above a picture the sign that indicates the appropriate activity.

**Teaching**
Have pupils turn to page 68 and locate the box containing a and A near the top of the page. Review the formation of a and introduce A as the capital form of the letter.
Ask pupils to look at the parts of the letter A as you give the following directions:
—Start at the top line; slant left down to the bottom line. Start at the same point on the top line; slant right down to the bottom line. Make a crossbar on the middle line.
[High start, slant left down. Same high start, slant right down. Cross.]

Emphasize that the cross stroke is written on the middle line. Repeat the directions as necessary while pupils trace and write the letter A on the first two lines.
Call attention to the lower-case letters. Tell pupils that these are the letters that they may refer to as they complete the page.
Discuss the pictures and labels below the lower-case letters. Bring out things pupils might see or do if they were to go to places like the ones pictured. Make sure children understand each label.

Instruct pupils to look at the first picture at the bottom of the page. Ask:
—Where are the children in this picture? (at an aquarium)
Instruct children to write a sign saying *Aquarium* above the picture. Allow children to continue writing the name of each place above each picture. Provide assistance on an individual basis if necessary.

**Activity**
*Signs.* Encourage children to think of places they have been to that have a sign at the door or gate. If the names of the suggested places are spelled with known capital letters, write them on the chalkboard. Give children a choice as to which sign they would like to write. Distribute paper and allow time for children to write and decorate their signs.

page 68

## Lesson 2

**Preparation.** The *Ahead of time* preparation gives the teacher hints for materials to have on hand or things to be done before class begins. The *Class time* preparation is generally a whole-group activity that provides a lead-in or preliminary practice for skills to be used on a page in the pupil's book.

### Lesson 2, page 69

**Objectives**
• Traces and writes manuscript letter *B*.
• Writes words and phrases that contain the letter *B*.

**Preparation**
*Ahead of time.* Be prepared to review any of the letters on page 69.

**Teaching** ▬▬▬▬▬

Have pupils turn to page 69 and locate the box near the top containing the letters *b* and *B*. Discuss the two letters, pointing out that *B* is very similar to *b*. The loops are on the same side in both letters. This observation may benefit those who reverse *b* and *d*.

Ask pupils to look at the parts of the *B* as you give the oral directions.

—Start at the top line; slant down to the bottom line; retrace up; go right around, down to the middle line, and close; go right around, down to the bottom line, and close.
[High start, down, up, around halfway, around again.]

Repeat the directions as necessary while pupils trace and write *B* on the lines.

Call attention to the capital and lower-case letters on the next line. Explain that pupils may refer to these letters as models while they complete the page.

Point out the sign that says *Beach* in the middle of the page. Tell students that the picture shows places where items may be purchased at this beach. Identify the names of these items with pupils.

Explain that pupils should write the name of each item they might like. Remind them to refer to the model letters above if they need help with letter formation.

Provide assistance to those students who need it. Most pupils should be able to proceed independently.

page 69

**Activity**
*Letter B Zoo.* Suggest that children think of names for animals that would appear in a zoo where all animals have names that begin with the letter *B*. You might want to start them off with names such as *Betty Bee, Buster Beetle,* and so on. Write the names on the board. Then let each child draw one of the animals and write the animal's name on a sheet of drawing paper.

Pupils see a comparison of capital and lower-case letter forms when each capital letter is introduced.

Children see a step-by-step visual sequence for making each letter.

Shaded letters provide tracing practice before children write letters on their own.

A letter model appears on the right and left sides of writing lines so that both left- and right-handed children will see a model as they write.

## Lesson 3

Plenty of space is provided for individual letter practice.

An activity immediately uses the new letter in words, phrases, or sentences.

Words, phrases, or sentences also appear in type.

**Lesson 3, page 70**

**Objectives**
- Traces and writes manuscript letter *D*.
- Writes a title and sentences that contain *D*.
- Adjusts space for first run-over sentence.

**Teaching**

Have pupils turn to page 70 and locate the box containing *d* and *D* at the top. Review the formation of the letter *d*, and explain that *D* is the capital form of that letter.

Ask pupils to look at the parts of the letter *D* as you give the following directions:
—Start at the top line; slant down to the bottom line; retrace up; curve right around, down to the bottom line, and close.
[High start down, up, around, and close.]

Repeat the directions as pupils begin to trace *D* and, if necessary, as they practice writing *D* on the writing lines.

Call attention to the picture of Doctor Dodge. Explain that *D* in *Doctor* is capitalized because *Doctor* is her title.

Read the sentence. Note with pupils that the *d* in *dentist* is not a capital within the sentence because it is not part of her title. Instruct pupils to trace the sentence, pointing out that it takes more than one line to write. Tell pupils to write the sentence on their own, using two lines and placing words just as they did when they traced the sentence.

Read the last sentence and ask pupils who is referred to by the word *She* (Doctor Dodge). Direct pupils to trace and write the sentence independently, paying close attention to letter formation and spacing.

**Special Populations**

Children with learning problems have trouble remembering which direction the letters *B*, *b*, *D*, and *d* should face. Capital *B* is remembered as having two humps on the side, while *D* has one hump. Lower-

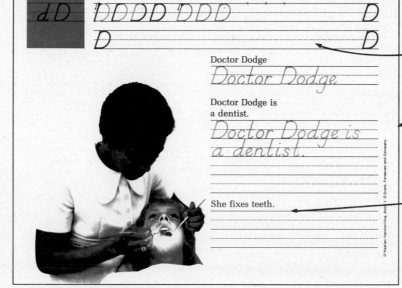

page 70

case *b* and *d* are very difficult to remember. In addition to emphasizing different starting points, you need to teach these children a physical memory technique for recalling *b* and *d*. Have the pupils make their hands into fists with each thumb pointing up. Help them imagine that the fleshy bulge beneath each thumb represents the round part of *b* or *d*. The left thumb stands for *b*, and the right thumb stands for *d*. On the chalkboard, write *bed* as a cue word.

By memorizing hand signals, children can remind themselves which way *b* and *d* face.

**Special Populations** section gives suggestions for helping children who are color-blind, left-handed, ambidextrous, immature, mirror-oriented, learning disabled, and so on. The hints may include specific teaching procedures or things to watch for in children's work.

# Lesson 4

**Activities** related to handwriting, motor coordination, or concepts are included in many lessons. The activities may be used for the whole class, for a handwriting center, or as additional work for children who finish ahead of the class.

**Extra lessons** occasionally give suggestions for preparing for an upcoming page, or for providing review and evaluation.

## Lesson 4, Review

### Objectives
- Reviews selected lower-case and capital letters.
- Reinforces concept that a capital letters is used as the first letter of the name of a public building or a street.
- Reinforces concept that the first letter of a name can be used as an initial.

### Preparation
*Ahead of time.* Have handwriting paper for each pupil. Select names of places pupils are familiar with that contain capital letters they have learned. *City Hall, Library,* and certain streets and avenues are some possibilities. If children have learned the capital letters in the name of their school, you might include that. Choose pupils' names containing known capital letters.
*Class time.* Distribute writing paper.

### Teaching, review
Tell children that they are going to learn to write names of places in their city or town. As you present the name of each place on the chalkboard, review the formation of letters—especially the capitals. Have children write the name on their paper.
Write the names of pupils you chose. Have children write the names, then underline the initials. If necessary, remind them that the first letter in each name is also an initial. If children seem to grasp this concept easily, you might include first and last names, asking pupils for two initials.

### Activity
*Letters come in all shapes and sizes.* Children may need to be reminded that letters do not always look the same. Demonstrate this to them by finding large examples of the same letter in several different type faces. Give children the opportunity to do the same thing. Provide them with magazines, scissors, paste, and paper. Let them volunteer for the letter they will look for. Encourage selection of varied letters, but caution children against selecting low-frequency letters, such as *Q.* If more than one child volunteers for the same letter, ask if the children would like to work together. Explain that they may search for both the lower-case and capital forms of their selected letter. When they cut out each letter, have them paste it on their paper. Advise children that the most varied type faces may be found in titles and ads. Display the completed collections of letters in alphabetical order.

## Other features

*D'Nealian*™ *Handwriting*, Book 1, reviews the readiness skills and introduces all manuscript letters, both capital and lower-case. Colorful pages teach handwriting skills and apply them to content areas and other "real-life" situations. Pages are self-contained, so elaborate equipment or other resources are not required.

## Letter order

In Book 1, all lower-case letters are taught first to enable most children to have a full alphabet at their command in four months or less. Since more than ninety percent of the letters children write are lower case, D'Nealian emphasizes this form before going on to the capital letters.

Letters are grouped for teaching by similarity of stroke—usually beginning stroke—to allow children to develop similar handwriting movements at one time.

The lower-case letters are taught in these groups:

    a  d  o  g  c  e  s
    f  b  l  t  h  k
    i  u  w  y  j  r  n  m  p
    q
    v  z  x

The capital letters are taught in these groups:

    C  G  O  Q  S
    I  L  T  J  U  H  K  A  B  D  M  N  P  R
    E  F  Z
    V  W  X  Y

Mathematics, page 25

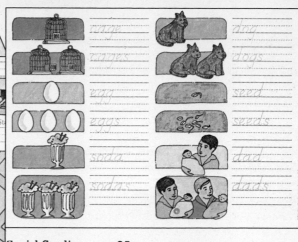

Language Arts, page 24

### Content areas

Pages in Book 1 deal with many activities that children encounter in school content areas. Numbers relate to skills for mathematics; capitalization, end-

Social Studies, page 95

ings, punctuation, and poetry form relate to language arts; classifying activities reinforce concepts for science; picture maps and path sequences build skills for social studies.

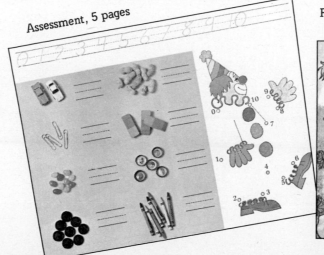

Assessment, 5 pages

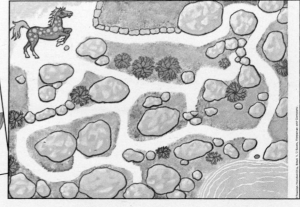

Review, 7 pages

### Assessment and review

An assessment and review section at the beginning of the book helps pupils and teachers find what help individuals need. Children who come to first grade

with little readiness for handwriting may benefit from some work in the Readiness book, which builds concepts, provides motor-coordination activities, and teaches numbers.

## Type models

In Book 1, the D'Nealian program takes responsibility for helping children learn to transcribe from print models. This procedure helps pupils cope with the many school and personal situations where they will have to write from a model that does not duplicate their handwriting.

Book 1 presents a printed word, a dark D'Nealian model, and a shaded tracing model for each word (see page 18).

The dark model is dropped from teaching pages as soon as children have some practice in tracing. Thereafter, only the printed word and the tracing model appear (see page 29).

Gradually, children are taught to write without a D'Nealian word model. Beginning on page 33, children are given printed words and D'Nealian letter models but must make their own D'Nealian word models.

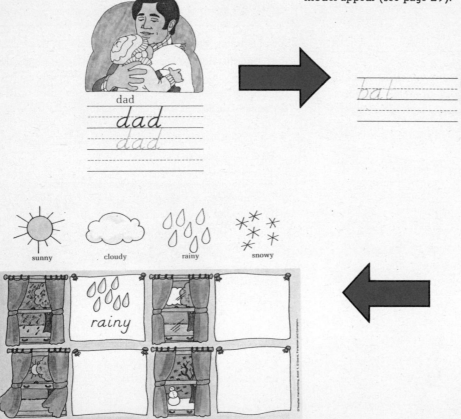

Finally, by page 98, pupils have their first page without D'Nealian models.

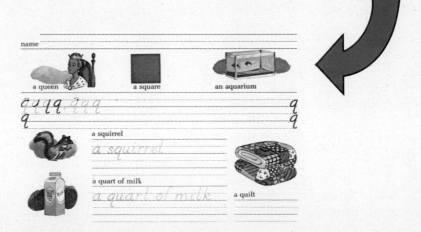

On page 47, the separate letter models do not appear, but the letters children need for the words a *quilt* appear in other words on the page.

# Hints for handwriting instruction

## Special helps

- Early supervision is important in teaching hand-writing. A paraprofessional, teacher's aide, or second teacher can be of particular help. While the teacher demonstrates from the front of the class, the second person can walk among children to check handwriting—particularly direction of stroke.
- If there are left-handed children in the class, learn to write left-handed at the chalkboard. This will help left-handed children visualize how a letter is formed "their way."
- Encourage children to cross out incorrect letters instead of erasing them. Young children tend to erase long and hard and are disappointed when their work is messy or has holes in it. By simply crossing out letters, pupils have neater papers and can see the mistakes they made.
- At the beginning of the year, give each child a D'Nealian model of his or her name. This may be on heavy paper or cardboard that can be propped up on a child's desk for reference.
- Set up a handwriting center in the classroom. You may want to have the following on hand:
  - paper and pencils in different sizes, textures, and colors;
  - magazines and newspapers for cutting;
  - a picture file with a picture for each capital and lower-case letter (people's names may be used for capital letters);
  - a chalkboard (individual chalkboards may be made by painting sturdy cardboard with chalk-board paint);
  - paste or white glue and things for gluing, such as fabric scraps, macaroni, glitter, buttons, string, and so on.

- Occasionally return messy or illegible papers to pupils for recopying to help establish the need for legibility and neatness in all handwriting that others are to read. This is especially important for work in content areas other than handwriting.
- Some children will try to do cursive writing in first grade. If children are so motivated (and you think they can handle it), they should be taught the correct way to make the transition. It is important not to let children experiment too much without guidance because they may form bad habits.

The transition is easy for most letters:

An uphill stroke is added at the beginning of these letters:

*e h i k l t u*

A beginning uphill stroke and a sidestroke or ending stroke are added to these letters:

*b j p w*

An overhill stroke is added at the beginning of these letters:

*a c d m n x y*

A beginning overhill stroke and a sidestroke or ending stroke are added to these letters:

*g o q*

These letters must be taught:

*f r s v z*

Letters that end like *h* naturally join letters that begin like *a*. Be careful to work with children on joinings for sidestroke letters. These involve changes in the beginning stroke of the letter that follows the sidestroke letter:

*on br vi wu*

Since most children making the transition at first grade will have plenty to handle with the lower-case letters, they probably will not be ready to learn cursive capitals. There is no harm in letting them use manuscript capital letters for a while.

## Paper

One-half-inch ruled paper with a midline is recommended for pupils in kindergarten through third grade. In *D'Nealian™ Handwriting*, Book 3, the midline is dropped toward the end of the book. One-third-inch ruled paper is recommended from fourth grade on. Basic instruction should be on paper of these sizes. A few individuals may show a strong preference for a different size. As long as a different size does not interfere with legibility or ease of writing, an individual may be permitted to use a size different from that used by others in the class.

It is, of course, useful at times to show children how different writing sizes can be used for different purposes—large for posters, small for mail-order forms, for example. The D'Nealian program specifically teaches children to deal with appropriate variations in size.

## Pencils

Medium-soft pencils are recommended for most handwriting work until children are well into middle grades. The erasability and friction of a pencil give better control than a pen for younger children. By sixth or seventh grade, children may begin using pens—fountain, ball-point, felt-tip.

The size pencil a child uses should be left to his or her preference. A variety of sizes should be available in the classroom—from tiny golf pencils to large primary pencils or crayons. Most children, even beginning writers, will be comfortable with a standard adult pencil, the type of pencil most children are accustomed to using in their homes.

## Position

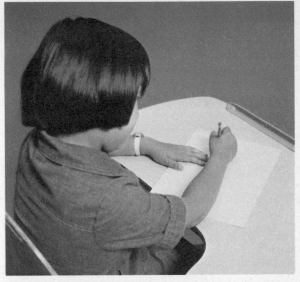

Paper position for a right-handed child.

The posture of children learning handwriting should be the same good posture essential to healthy body growth. Children should sit tall, with both feet on the floor and arms relaxed on a table or desk. Children who slump over their desks or sit back on their tailbones cannot do their best work.

Paper should be positioned at a slant for both manuscript and cursive writing. The slant of the paper should approximately parallel the writing arm. For left-handed children, the paper should slant from the right at the top to the left at the bottom (approximately the two-o'clock position). The right-handed child should slant the paper from the left at the top to the right at the bottom (approximately the ten-o'clock position).

Paper position for a left-handed child.

Children should grasp their pencils lightly between the thumb and index finger, usually about an inch above the pencil point. The index finger should rest on the top of the pencil, and the pencil should be supported on the first joint of the middle finger. This pencil position is the same for left- and right-handed children, except that left-handed children may be more comfortable grasping the pencil farther from the point.

Often a child who holds the pencil too tightly also grasps it too close to the point. A simple remedy is to wrap a rubber band around the pencil about an inch above the point. The child should hold the pencil above the rubber band.

Pencil position for a left-handed child.

Pencil position for a right-handed child.

## Special transition problems

Many schools will have children transferring into their classes from schools that have not taught D'Nealian. Should these children learn D'Nealian?

The answer depends on the child. Because the authors of D'Nealian place their emphases on legibility and individuality, they believe a child who has been doing superior work with another method—even the circle and straight line method—should not be forced to change to D'Nealian. On the other hand, most children who are doing poor work with another method should be strongly encouraged to learn D'Nealian. Its simplicity is particularly useful for children having difficulty with other methods.

If young transfer students maintain their old method of manuscript writing instead of learning D'Nealian manuscript, they will need extra help making the transition to cursive. These children most likely will not have established the form, size, slant, and rhythm necessary for cursive writing.

*a* Start at the middle line; go left around, down to the bottom line, around and up to the beginning; close; retrace down, and swing up.
[Around, down, up, down, and a monkey tail.]

*b* Start at the top line; slant down to the bottom line; go right around, up to the middle line; curve left and close.
[High start, down, around, up into a tummy.]

*c* Start a little below the middle line; go up to the middle line; go left around, down to the bottom line; curve right and stop.
[Curved start, around, down, up, and stop.]

*d* Start at the middle line; go left around, down to the bottom line, around up to the top line; retrace down, and swing up.
[Around, down, up high, down, and a monkey tail.]

*e* Start between the middle and bottom lines; curve right up to the middle line; go left around, down to the bottom line; curve right and stop.
[Curve up, around, down, up, and stop.]

*f* Start a little below the top line; go up to the top line; go left around, slant down to the bottom line. Make a crossbar on the middle line.
[Curved high start, around, down. Cross.]

*g* Start at the middle line; go left around, down to the bottom line, around up to the middle line; close; retrace down, and go half a line below the bottom line; hook to the left.
[Around, down, up, down, and a fishhook under water.]

*h* Start at the top line; slant down to the bottom line; retrace up halfway; make a hump to the right, and swing up.
[High start, down, up, and a hump with a monkey tail.]

*i* Start at the middle line; slant down to the bottom line, and swing up. Make a dot above the letter.
[Down, and a monkey tail. Add a dot.]

*j* Start at the middle line; slant down half a line below the bottom line; hook to the left. Make a dot above the letter.
[Down, and a fishhook under water. Add a dot.]

*k* Start at the top line; slant down to the bottom line; retrace up halfway; make a loop to the right and close; slant right to the bottom line, and swing up.
[High start, down, up, small tummy, and a monkey tail.]

*l* Start at the top line; slant down to the bottom line, and swing up.
[High start, down, and a monkey tail.]

*m* Start at the middle line; slant down to the bottom line; retrace up to the middle line; make a hump to the right; slant down to the bottom line; retrace up; make another hump to the right; slant down to the bottom line, and swing up.
[Down, up, hump, hump, and a monkey tail.]

*n* Start at the middle line; slant down to the bottom line; retrace up to the middle line; make a hump to the right; slant down to the bottom line, and swing up.
[Down, up, hump, and a monkey tail].

*o* Start at the middle line; go left around, down to the bottom line, around and up to the beginning; close.
[Around, down, up, and close.]

*p* Start at the middle line; slant down half a line below the bottom line; retrace up; go right around, down to the bottom line, and close.
[Down under water, up, around, and a tummy.]

*q* Start at the middle line; go left around, down to the bottom line, around and up to the beginning; close; retrace down, and go half a line below the bottom line; hook to the right.
[Around, down, up, down, and a backward fishhook under water.]

*r* Start at the middle line; slant down to the bottom line; retrace up; make a hump to the right, and stop.
[Down, up, and a roof.]

*s* Start a little below the middle line; go up to the middle line; go left around, down halfway; then go right around, down to the bottom line; curve left and stop.
[Curved start, around left, and a snake tail.]

*t* Start at the top line; slant down to the bottom line and swing up. Make a crossbar on the middle line.
[High start, down, and a monkey tail. Cross.]

*u* Start at the middle line; slant down to the bottom line; curve right; slant up to the middle line; retrace down, and swing up.
[Down, over, up, down, and a monkey tail.]

*v* Start at the middle line; slant right down to the bottom line; slant right up to the middle line.
[Slant right down, slant right up.]

*w* Start at the middle line; slant down to the bottom line; curve right; slant up to the middle line; retrace down; curve right; slant up to the middle line.
[Down, over, up, down, over, up.]

*x* Start at the middle line; slant right down to the bottom line, and swing up. Cross the letter with a slant left.
[Slant down and a monkey tail. Cross with a slant.]

*y* Start at the middle line; slant down to the bottom line; curve right; slant up to the middle line; retrace down, and go half a line below the bottom line; hook to the left.
[Down, over, up, down under water, and a fishhook.]

*z* Start at the middle line; make a bar to the right on the middle line; slant left down to the bottom line; make a bar to the right on the bottom line.
[Over, slant down, over.]

Start at the top line; slant left down to the bottom line. Start at the same point on the top line; slant right down to the bottom line. Make a crossbar on the middle line.
[High start, slant left down. Same high start, slant right down. Cross.]

 Start at the top line; slant down to the bottom line; retrace up; go right around, down to the middle line, and close; go right around, down to the bottom line, and close.
[High start, down, up, around halfway, around again.]

Start a little below the top line; go up to the top line, go left around, down to the bottom line; curve right and stop.
[Curved high start, around, down, up, and stop.]

Start at the top line; slant down to the bottom line; retrace up; curve right around, down to the bottom line, and close.
[High start down, up, around, and close.]

 Start at the top line; make a bar to the left on the top line; slant down to the bottom line; make a bar to the right. Start at the middle of the letter; make a bar to the right.
[High start, over left, down, over right. Middle bar across.]

Start at the top line; make a bar to the left on the top line; slant down to the bottom line. Start at the middle of the letter; make a bar to the right.
[High start, over left, down. Middle bar across.]

Start a little below the top line; go up to the top line; go left around, down to the bottom line; curve right, up to the middle line; make a bar to the left.
[Curved high start, around, down, up, and over left.]

 Start at the top line; slant down to the bottom line. Start at the top line, to the right of the first start; slant down to the bottom line. Make a crossbar on the middle line.
[High start, down. High start, down. Middle bar across.]

 Start at the top line; slant down to the bottom line. Make a small crossbar on the top line. Make a small crossbar on the bottom line.
[Down. Cross top. Cross bottom.]

 Start at the top line; slant down to the bottom line; curve left and stop.
[High start, down, and curve up left.]

 Start at the top line; slant down to the bottom line. Start at the top line, to the right of the first start; slant left down to the middle line, and join; slant right down to the bottom line, and swing up.
[High start, down. High start, slant halfway, slant down, and a monkey tail.]

 Start at the top line; slant down to the bottom line; make a bar to the right.
[High start, down and over right.]

 Start at the top line; slant down to the bottom line. Start at the same point on the top line; slant right, down to the middle line; slant right, up to the top line; slant down to the bottom line.
[High start, down. Same high start, slant down halfway, slant up, down.]

 Start at the top line; slant down to the bottom line. Start at the same point on the top line; slant right, down to the bottom line; go up to the top line.
[High start, down. Same high start, slant down, up.]

 Start at the top line; go left around, down to the bottom line, around and up to the beginning; close.
[Curved high start, around, down, up, and close.]

 Start at the top line; slant down to the bottom line; retrace up; go right around, down to the middle line, and close.
[High start, down, up, around, halfway, and close.]

 Start at the top line; go left around, down to the bottom line, around and up to the beginning; close. Start below the middle line; slant right across the bottom of the letter, and swing up.
[Curved high start, around, down, up, close. Add a monkey tail.]

Start at the top line; slant down to the bottom line; retrace up; go right around, down to the middle line, and close; slant right down to the bottom line, and swing up.
[High start, down, up, around halfway, slant down, and a monkey tail.]

Start a little below the top line; go up to the top line; go left around, down to the middle line; then go right around, down to the bottom line; curve left, up, and stop.
[Curved high start, around left, and a snake tail.]

Start at the top line; slant down to the bottom line. Make a crossbar on the top line.
[High start, down. Cross.]

Start at the top line; slant down to the bottom line; curve right; slant up to the top line; retrace down, and swing up.
[High start, down, over, up high, down, and a monkey tail.]

Start at the top line; slant right down to the bottom line; slant right up to the top line.
[Slant right down; slant right up.]

Start at the top line; slant right down to the bottom line; slant right up to the top line; slant right down to the bottom line; slant right up to the top line.
[High start, slant right down, slant right up, slant right down, slant right up.]

Start at the top line; slant right down to the bottom line, and swing up. Cross the letter with a slant left.
[High start, slant right down, and a monkey tail. Cross.]

Start at the top line; slant right down to the middle line. Start at the top line, to the right of the first start; slant left down, join the first slant at the middle line, and go down to the bottom line.
[High start, slant right halfway. High start, slant left down.]

Start at the top line; make a bar to the right on the top line; slant left down to the bottom line; make a bar to the right.
[Over right, slant left down, over right.]

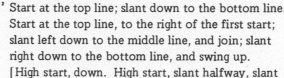
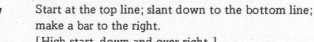

# Problems in Classroom Learning

by Dale R. Jordan

It is beyond any teacher's power to diagnose and remediate all problems encountered in classroom teaching. However, being aware of the major clues that signal when a child cannot cope with certain tasks can help the teacher modify daily expectations.

Clues to five problems are particularly likely to become apparent during handwriting instruction. These clues relate to immaturity for learning, poor visual control for near work, and three forms of learning disability (poor visual memory, poor auditory memory, and dysgraphia—difficulty controlling handwriting muscles to write correctly).

## Immaturity for learning

The key to classroom success is reduction of frustration in both the child and the teacher. Recognizing whether a child is mature enough to learn can reduce stress that triggers frustration. Primary-classroom teachers see many immature children, especially when birthdays come near the beginning of the school year. The younger the beginner, the more likelihood there is that delayed maturity will interfere with classroom learning.

Certain maturity signals are evident to an observant teacher. The following skills indicate that a child is ready for handwriting:
—good control of pencil, crayons, scissors, and buttons and zippers on clothing;
—ability to follow a series of instructions without forgetting;
—ability to match corners in folding paper;
—ability to stay within the lines while coloring;
—ability to copy simple shapes successfully;
—certainty as to which hand to use.

## Poor visual control for near work

As yet we have no explanation for the increasing numbers of children who manifest poor vision for sustained near work in school. The traditional standard for school vision has been the Snellen eye chart, which yields a ratio (20/20, 20/30, and so on). This vision standard is based upon what a child can see from a distance of twenty feet. It has virtually no bearing upon what the pupil can see at eighteen inches, where most of a child's daily classroom vision must remain focused. Most primary pupils are farsighted. It is easier for them to focus clearly on the chalkboard across the room than to hold clear focus for several minutes at desk-top distance. Many children do poor classroom work because they do not see well for near work. If the eyes do not remain coordinated during near work at desk-top level, the pupil quickly becomes restless, loses the place, and has trouble staying on the line.

A child's handwriting provides clues of poor visual control for near work. The following behaviors usually signal poor vision for paper-and-pencil work:
—cannot place finger on a given place on the page;
—writing continues to be too large for the work space provided on the page;
—uneven spacing appears with wide gaps between letters, or letters bunched too close together;
—complains of headache during sustained near work;
—begins to squint soon after starting to copy from the chalkboard;
—leans very close to paper;
—continually changes posture while writing (leans sideways, leans back, sits on one foot);
—quality of writing deteriorates significantly as work continues.

Of course not all children with these behaviors have vision problems, but a majority of the pupils who manifest these symptoms have poor visual control for sustained writing at a flat-topped desk.

## Learning disability

During the past decade educators have made an alarming discovery. Approximately fifteen percent of those who fail in school are learning disabled. This figure represents several million youngsters currently enrolled in school, along with millions of adults already in the labor market.

The eminent European educator Jean Piaget provided a framework for understanding how pupils master academic skills when he proposed the concept of *conservation of form*. This means that a child must be able to hold memory patterns intact in order to succeed in school. The child must conserve many kinds of form. What is seen (visual form) must be preserved somehow through memory strategies so it can be recalled later and used to solve problems. What the child hears (auditory form) must be preserved for future use in connection with what was seen. What a child experiences through touch and body movement (tactile and kinesthetic form) must blend with what is seen and heard to form memory patterns that the child uses later to solve problems. To succeed in school, a child must be able to conserve form and to combine several forms into meaningful memory structures.

"Learning disability" is the general term used to identify the child who cannot conserve standard form.

## Poor visual memory

One of the cornerstones for classroom success is creating mental pictures of what is seen. A child must pay close attention to all details of what is seen, then somehow store up that visual image for later use. The learning-disabled child seldom has accurate recall of what was seen. Visual memory, which is distorted by confused directionality, is manifested by reversed numerals in the number line or reversed letters in writing the alphabet.

Success in the American educational framework rests upon the assumption that all children learn in a specific directional way: left-to-right and top-to-bottom. Reading, writing, spelling, recalling information in sequence, history facts, scientific formulas, and similar academic work proceed left to right, top to bottom, or a combination of these directions.

Left-to-right awareness is especially important in handwriting. Failure to work left to right causes reversed letters and poor writing. At least fifteen percent of the students in our schools do not develop this directional orientation. Virtually every classroom in America includes learners who tend to work backwards. The term "mirror image" or "mirror orientation" is often applied to this reversed learning orientation (which is outgrown by some children).

It is very difficult for the mirror child to establish left-and-right awareness. These directional guideposts are constantly transposed within the child's memory structure. Occasionally top and bottom become reversed, further complicating the child's learning dilemma. If the teacher presents to the class the letter *d*, the mirror child usually perceives *b*. If the teacher presents the word *saw*, the mirror child perceives it as *was*. If the teacher asks the pu-pils to put their fingers on the top left corner of the page, the mirror child touches the opposite side.

In virtually every instance involving directionality, the learning-disabled child's response is labeled "wrong." Inwardly the pupil believes his or her understanding to be correct, but adults constantly say, "You did it wrong." The confused child becomes highly frustrated and eventually rejects school learning because of constant failure and criticism.

The following learning characteristics are manifested by children with faulty visual memory:
—confusion with left and right;
—confusion with place concepts (over and under; before and after; first, next, last; and so on);
—difficulty learning information in a given sequence (alphabet, number line, multiplication tables, phone numbers, house numbers, own birth date, days of the week, months of the year, seasons of the year, and so on);
—reversal of letters (*b* and *d*, *p* and *q*) or rotation of symbols (*b* and *p*, *d* and *q*, 6 and 9, 7 and *L*, *n* and *u*, *M* and *W*, *N* and *Z*);
—mirror reading (*was* for *saw*, *on* for *no*, 13 for 31);
—need to subvocalize (whisper to self) while writing information in sequence (must go back to the beginning and say the whole sequence to write the next element of a memorized sequence);
—confusion of likeness and difference.

## Poor auditory memory

The most frustrating form of learning disability involves faulty retention of what the pupil hears. In most cases, nothing is wrong with the child's hearing as such. Information gained through hearing is passed into the memory systems. At that point a breakdown occurs for some children. What the child hears does not trigger memory for what the words mean. Even when the child knows each word in isolation, the overall meaning does not register when continuous speech is experienced. Most children who manifest this syndrome fully comprehend less than half of what they hear. In most cases of faulty auditory memory, the child fully understands only twenty to thirty percent of the total listening input.

Not only does the child not attach meaning to the words picked up by hearing, he or she does not retain the sequence. Even when full understanding occurs, the sequence immediately scrambles, causing the child to lose the mental image that was built through careful listening. This leaves the child with a bewildering set of options. The student can bluff, pretending to have understood what the teacher told the group to do. Sooner or later this technique fails, usually ending in a reprimand because the teacher does not know the reason for the bluff. Or the child can glean bits and pieces of what to do from other students. This usually backfires with a scolding, especially if the teacher has warned pupils not to help each other do their work. Or the frustrated child can do nothing, always pleading, "I didn't understand what I was supposed to do." While this is actually true, few adults believe such a story time after time after time. Another option is available. The child with low auditory perception can panic or rebel, creating a disturbance that momentarily takes the teacher's mind off the task which the child does not comprehend. None of these are productive options, of course, but they are all that most learning-disabled children can exercise.

A handwriting problem seen in most cases of poor auditory memory is the inability to associate sounds with symbols quickly enough to keep up with dictation. If given enough time to rehearse and use trial-and-error, a child with poor auditory memory frequently can arrive at correct spellings, but not fast enough to keep up with the class during dictation. This is especially true when teachers incorporate spelling words within dictated sentences, giving the class limited time to write what the teacher dictates. The term *auditory-to-motor* is used to describe the task of hearing a spoken pattern, quickly connecting what is heard with what has been learned previously about sound-symbol relationships, then putting on paper what the teacher expects. Writing from dictation or from one's own inner voice is virtually impossible for the child with deficient auditory perception.

The following behaviors are characteristic of the child with faulty auditory perception (poor auditory memory):
—never has enough time when writing from dictation;
—constantly erases and tries again, using trial-and-error rehearsal until it looks right;
—cannot follow the sequence of oral instructions given by teacher;
—frequently transposes consonants while writing (*brid* for *bird; bran* for *barn*);
—tries to pick up clues from other pupils, or tries to bluff.

## Dysgraphia

Often, but not always, associated with poor visual and auditory memory is the difficulty many children have controlling handwriting muscles to write correctly what the child is thinking. Dysgraphia involves loss of directionality along with loss of mental images as the pencil touches the paper. The problem seems to be that a "short-circuit effect" occurs during the physical act of putting mental images into written form.

Dysgraphia involves backward handstrokes, actually turning the hand in a reversed direction during the act of writing. Children who are dysgraphic usually write with heavy pressure which leaves a smudged, messy finished product. Often classroom grades are awarded for neatness. This leaves the dysgraphic child out in the cold. To make legible symbols at all, the dysgraphic pupil must put forth a slow, painstaking effort. In spite of best intentions, he or she reverses circular symbols, marking clockwise, which is backwards. Cursive writing experience tends to clear up the more obvious signals of dysgraphia, but upon close examination the observer may see that the cursive handwriting is actually a series of isolated bits and pieces strung together.

A dysgraphic child faces problems with figure-ground control in writing. This refers to the business of keeping regular spacing between words or separate symbols. Problems with figure-ground control also become apparent when children must number paper according to oral instructions. Dysgraphic students find it difficult to number every other line. They quickly lose the spacing rhythm of a task. They become highly frustrated with written projects. They usually respond well to spacing techniques, such as laying down one or two fingers before writing the next word, but not if they are pressed to write in a hurry.

Symptoms of dysgraphia include the following behaviors:
—backward handstrokes (reversed circles, marking bottom to top);
—very labored writing, usually with heavy pressure on pencil;
—constant loss of figure-ground control, especially in numbering lines;
—much erasing, then making the same mistakes again and again.

These, then, are the principal causes for classroom failure: delayed maturity, poor vision for near work, faulty visual memory in which symbols reverse and rotate, poor understanding through listening, and difficulty putting what one knows into correct written form. The teacher's responsibility is to be watchful for the signals. While no teacher can solve all of these learning problems, knowledge of why a child behaves in a particular way will allow the teacher to reduce pressure and modify daily work expectations. Children who manifest these symptoms should be referred to appropriate specialists for further evaluation.

# Scope and Sequence Chart

▨ skill introduced;  ▦ skill maintained.

| | Readiness | Grade 1 | Grade 2 | Grade 3 | Grade 4 | Grade 5 | Grade 6 | Grade 7 | Grade 8 |
|---|---|---|---|---|---|---|---|---|---|
| **I. Preparing for handwriting** | | | | | | | | | |
| A. Concepts and terminology | | | | | | | | | |
|   1. Location and direction | | | | | | | | | |
|     a. above-below | introduced | maintained | maintained | maintained | | | | | |
|     b. around | introduced | maintained | maintained | maintained | | | | | |
|     c. first, next, last | introduced | maintained | maintained | maintained | | | | | |
|     d. left-right | introduced | maintained | maintained | maintained | | | | | |
|     e. start-stop | introduced | maintained | maintained | maintained | | | | | |
|     f. top, middle, bottom | introduced | maintained | maintained | maintained | | | | | |
|     g. up-down; over-under | introduced | maintained | maintained | maintained | | | | | |
|   2. Relationships | | | | | | | | | |
|     a. alike, different | introduced | maintained | maintained | maintained | | | | | |
|     b. classifying | introduced | maintained | maintained | maintained | | | | | |
|     c. place | introduced | maintained | maintained | maintained | | | | | |
|     d. sequence | introduced | maintained | maintained | maintained | | | | | |
|     e. size | introduced | maintained | maintained | maintained | | | | | |
|   3. Forms of communication | | | | | | | | | |
|     a. pictures | introduced | maintained | | | | | | | |
|     b. language | | | | | | | | | |
|      (1) spoken | introduced | maintained | | | | | | | |
|      (2) written | introduced | maintained | | | | | | | |
| B. Perceptual skills | | | | | | | | | |
|   1. Visual discrimination | | | | | | | | | |
|     a. alignment (on line) | introduced | maintained | maintained | | | | | | |
|     b. color | introduced | maintained | maintained | | | | | | |
|     c. shape | introduced | maintained | maintained | | | | | | |
|     d. size | introduced | maintained | maintained | | | | | | |
|   2. Auditory perception | | | | | | | | | |
|     a. following oral directions | introduced | maintained | | | | | | | |
|     b. listening | introduced | maintained | | | | | | | |
| C. Motor coordination | | | | | | | | | |
|   1. eye-hand | introduced | maintained | maintained | | | | | | |
|   2. fine motor | introduced | maintained | maintained | | | | | | |
|   3. large motor | introduced | maintained | maintained | | | | | | |
|   4. rhythm | introduced | maintained | maintained | | | | | | |
|   5. handwriting position | introduced | maintained | maintained | | | | | | |
| **II. Learning handwriting** | | | | | | | | | |
| A. Elements of written communication | | | | | | | | | |
|   1. Numbers, letters, and words | | | | | | | | | |
|     a. numbers | | | | | | | | | |
|      (1) 0-10 | introduced | maintained | maintained | maintained | maintained | maintained | maintained | maintained | maintained |
|      (2) greater than 10 | | | introduced | maintained | maintained | maintained | maintained | maintained | maintained |
|      (3) decimals | | | | | introduced | maintained | maintained | maintained | maintained |
|      (4) names for numbers | | introduced | maintained | maintained | maintained | maintained | maintained | maintained | maintained |
|      (5) ordinals | | | | introduced | maintained | maintained | | | |
|      (6) Roman numerals | | | | | | introduced | maintained | | |

# Scope and Sequence Chart

▓ skill introduced;  ░ skill maintained.

| | Readiness | Grade 1 | Grade 2 | Grade 3 | Grade 4 | Grade 5 | Grade 6 | Grade 7 | Grade 8 |
|---|---|---|---|---|---|---|---|---|---|
| b. manuscript letters | | | | | | | | | |
| (1) lower case | | | | | | | | | |
| a, d, o, g, c, e, s; | * | ▓ | ░ | ░ | ░ | ░ | ░ | ░ | ░ |
| f, b, l, t, h, k; | * | ▓ | ░ | ░ | ░ | ░ | ░ | ░ | ░ |
| i, u, w, y, j, r, n, m, p; | * | ▓ | ░ | ░ | ░ | ░ | ░ | ░ | ░ |
| q, v, z, x. | * | ▓ | ░ | ░ | ░ | ░ | ░ | ░ | ░ |
| (2) capital | | | | | | | | | |
| C, G, O, Q, S; | * | ▓ | ░ | ░ | ░ | ░ | ░ | ░ | ░ |
| I, L, T, J, U, H, K, | * | ▓ | ░ | ░ | ░ | ░ | ░ | ░ | ░ |
| A, B, D, M, N, P, R; | * | ▓ | ░ | ░ | ░ | ░ | ░ | ░ | ░ |
| E, F, C; | * | ▓ | ░ | ░ | ░ | ░ | ░ | ░ | ░ |
| V, W, X, Y. | * | ▓ | ░ | ░ | ░ | ░ | ░ | ░ | ░ |
| c. cursive letters | | | | | | | | | |
| (1) lower case | | | | | | | | | |
| l, h, k, t; | | | ▓ | ░ | ░ | ░ | ░ | ░ | ░ |
| i, u, e, j; | | | ▓ | ░ | ░ | ░ | ░ | ░ | ░ |
| a, d, c, m, n, x; | | | ▓ | ░ | ░ | ░ | ░ | ░ | ░ |
| g, y, q; | | | ▓ | ░ | ░ | ░ | ░ | ░ | ░ |
| p, o, w, b, s, r, f, z, v. | | | ▓ | ░ | ░ | ░ | ░ | ░ | ░ |
| (2) capital | | | | | | | | | |
| A, C, E, O; | | | ▓ | ░ | ░ | ░ | ░ | ░ | ░ |
| H, K, M, N, U, V, W, Y; | | | ▓ | ░ | ░ | ░ | ░ | ░ | ░ |
| T, F; | | | ▓ | ░ | ░ | ░ | ░ | ░ | ░ |
| B, P, R; | | | ▓ | ░ | ░ | ░ | ░ | ░ | ░ |
| G, S, I; | | | ▓ | ░ | ░ | ░ | ░ | ░ | ░ |
| Z, Q; | | | ▓ | ░ | ░ | ░ | ░ | ░ | ░ |
| D, J, X, L. | | | ▓ | ░ | ░ | ░ | ░ | ░ | ░ |
| (3) joining strokes | | | ▓ | ░ | ░ | ░ | ░ | ░ | ░ |
| d. words | | ▓ | ░ | ░ | ░ | ░ | ░ | ░ | ░ |
| 2. Sentences and paragraphs | | | | | | | | | |
| a. form | | ▓ | ░ | ░ | ░ | ░ | ░ | ░ | ░ |
| b. punctuation | | | | | | | | | |
| (1) apostrophe | | | | | | | | | |
| (a) possessive | | ▓ | ░ | ░ | ░ | ░ | ░ | ░ | ░ |
| (b) contraction | | | ▓ | | ░ | ░ | ░ | ░ | ░ |
| (2) colon | | | ▓ | ░ | ░ | ░ | ░ | ░ | ░ |
| (3) comma | | | ▓ | ░ | ░ | ░ | ░ | ░ | ░ |
| (4) exclamation mark | | | | ▓ | ░ | ░ | ░ | ░ | ░ |
| (5) hyphen | | | | | ▓ | ░ | ░ | ░ | ░ |
| (6) parentheses | | | | | | | | ▓ | ░ |
| (7) period | | ▓ | ░ | ░ | ░ | ░ | ░ | ░ | ░ |
| (8) question mark | | ▓ | ░ | ░ | ░ | ░ | ░ | ░ | ░ |
| (9) quotation marks | | | | | ▓ | ░ | ░ | ░ | ░ |
| (10) semicolon | | | | ▓ | | ░ | ░ | ░ | |
| (11) other (brackets, dash, etc.) | | | ▓ | ░ | ░ | ░ | ░ | ░ | ░ |

* The option is available for teaching letters at the Readiness level.

# Scope and Sequence Chart

▓ skill introduced;  ░ skill maintained.

| | Readiness | Grade 1 | Grade 2 | Grade 3 | Grade 4 | Grade 5 | Grade 6 | Grade 7 | Grade 8 |
|---|---|---|---|---|---|---|---|---|---|
| c. capitalization | | | | | | | | | |
|   (1) names | | I | M | M | M | M | M | M | M |
|   (2) first word in sentence | | I | M | M | M | M | M | M | M |
|   (3) abbreviations and initials | | I | M | M | M | M | M | M | M |
|   (4) acronyms | | | | | | I | | | |
| 3. Symbols | | | | | | | | | |
|   a. computation | | | | | | | | | |
|     (1) addition | | | | | I | M | M | M | M |
|     (2) subtraction | | | | | I | M | M | M | M |
|     (3) multiplication | | | | | | I | M | | M |
|   b. direction and other (money; metric) | | | I | | M | M | M | M | M |
| B. Appropriate variations | | | | | | | | | |
|   1. Style | | | | | | | | | |
|     a. signature | | | I | M | M | M | M | M | M |
|     b. ornamentation | | | | | | | I | | |
|     c. block letters | | | | | | | | | |
|   2. Purpose | | | | | | | | | |
|     a. size | | | I | M | M | M | M | M | M |
|     b. speed | | | | | | | I | M | M |
|     c. format | | | | | | | | | |
|       (1) margins | | | I | M | M | M | M | M | M |
|       (2) writing without lines | | I | M | M | M | M | M | M | M |
| C. Evaluation | | | | | | | | | |
|   1. Criteria for legibility | | | | | | | | | |
|     a. form | I | M | M | M | M | M | M | M | M |
|     b. consistency | | | | | | | | | |
|       (1) slant | I | M | M | M | M | M | M | M | M |
|       (2) size | I | M | M | M | M | M | M | M | M |
|       (3) spacing | I | M | M | M | M | M | M | M | M |
|   2. Methods of evaluation | | | | | | | | | |
|     a. teacher | I | M | M | M | M | M | M | M | M |
|     b. pupil | I | M | M | M | M | M | M | M | M |
| III. Using handwriting | | | | | | | | | |
| A. School content areas | | | | | | | | | |
|   1. Health and safety | I | M | M | M | M | M | M | | M |
|   2. Language arts | I | M | M | M | M | M | M | M | M |
|   3. Mathematics | I | M | M | M | M | M | M | M | M |
|   4. Science | I | M | M | M | | M | M | M | M |
|   5. Social studies | | I | M | M | M | M | M | M | M |
| B. Individual learning | | | | | | | | | |
|   1. Note taking | | | | | | | I | | |
|   2. Outlining | | | | | | I | M | | |
|   3. Using resource materials | | | | | | | | | |
|     a. atlas | | | | | | | I | | |
|     b. card catalog | | | | | | I | M | | |
|     c. chart | | | I | M | M | M | M | M | M |

# Scope and Sequence Chart

▓▓▓ skill introduced;   ░░░ skill maintained.

| | Readiness | Grade 1 | Grade 2 | Grade 3 | Grade 4 | Grade 5 | Grade 6 | Grade 7 | Grade 8 |
|---|---|---|---|---|---|---|---|---|---|
| d. diagram | | | | introduced | maintained | maintained | maintained | | maintained |
| e. dictionary | | | | | introduced | maintained | | maintained | |
| f. encyclopedia | | | | | | | | | |
| g. map | | | introduced | maintained | maintained | maintained | maintained | maintained | maintained |
| h. schedule | | | | | | | introduced | | |
| i. table | | | | | | introduced | maintained | | maintained |
| j. thesaurus | | | | | | | introduced | maintained | |
| **4. Critical thinking** | | | | | | | | | |
| a. bias and propaganda | | | | | introduced | | maintained | | |
| b. fact vs. opinion | | | | | | introduced | | | maintained |
| c. connotations of words | | | | | introduced | | maintained | | |
| d. reality vs. fantasy | | | | introduced | | | | | |
| **C. Recreation** | | | | | | | | | |
| 1. Art and crafts | introduced | maintained | maintained | maintained | maintained | maintained | maintained | maintained | maintained |
| 2. Games | introduced | maintained | | maintained | maintained | maintained | maintained | maintained | maintained |
| **D. Correspondence** | | | | | | | | | |
| 1. Business | | | | | | | | | |
| a. bills, checks | | | | | | | introduced | | maintained |
| b. queries, complaints | | | | | | introduced | | | maintained |
| c. orders | | | | | introduced | | | maintained | maintained |
| 2. Personal | | | | | | | | | |
| a. invitations | | | introduced | | maintained | | | maintained | maintained |
| b. letters, notes | | | introduced | maintained | maintained | maintained | maintained | maintained | maintained |
| c. lists | | introduced | maintained | maintained | maintained | maintained | maintained | maintained | maintained |
| d. messages | | | | introduced | | | maintained | maintained | maintained |
| e. other | | | | introduced | | | | | maintained |
| **E. Career applications** | | | | | | | | | |
| 1. Forms | | | | | | | | | |
| a. applications | | | | | | | introduced | | maintained |
| b. orders | | | | | introduced | maintained | | maintained | maintained |
| c. other (want ads, calling cards) | | | | | introduced | | maintained | | |
| 2. Record keeping | | | | | | | | | |
| a. journal | | | | | | | | introduced | maintained |
| b. chart | | | | | | | | introduced | |
| c. other (library card) | | | | introduced | | | | maintained | |
| 3. Labeling | | introduced | maintained | maintained | maintained | maintained | maintained | maintained | maintained |

# SECTION 1

## pages 5, 6, 7, 8

## Lesson 1, page 5

### Objectives

- Marks pictured objects to show that they are the same.
- Marks a pictured object to show that it is in the *middle* of two other objects.

### Preparation

*Class time.* Distribute a crayon and a handwriting book to each child. Allow pupils time to look through the book.

### Teaching

When pupils have examined the book, help them locate page 5. Explain that they will have to listen very closely to the instructions you give them to complete this page.

Call attention to the left side of the page, containing the pictures of the chest of drawers and three toy bears. Assist any children who are having difficulty locating the pictures. Instruct pupils as follows:

—Look at the picture of the drawers. Color the one that is in the middle.
—Look at the pictures of the toy bears. Color the one that is in the middle.

Next, call attention to the upper right-hand corner, containing the pictures of the three snowmen and the clocks. Instruct pupils to listen carefully as you give the following directions.

—Look at the pictures of the three snowmen. Find the two that are the same and mark them. [Use any

name

marking procedure that children are familiar with—circling, underlining, or the like.]
—Now look carefully at the pictures of the three clocks. Mark the two that are the same. Later, evaluate pupils' responses to determine their understanding of the concepts tested on the page. You may wish to note individuals who need review of likenesses and differences, or positions (top, middle, bottom).

## Objectives
- Develops visual discrimination by matching colors and shapes of objects.
- Colors a shape a specific color.

## Preparation
*Ahead of time.* Have a red, yellow, blue, green, and brown crayon for each child or for a small group of children.

*Class time.* To review colors, hold up a red crayon and let a volunteer tell what color it is. Follow the same procedure with a yellow, a blue, an orange, a green, and a brown crayon.

## Teaching
Have pupils turn to page 6 and look at the first shape at the top of the page. Have a volunteer tell what color it is (red). Then ask pupils to find shapes on the page that are exactly like the red one. Tell pupils they are to use a red crayon to color everything which is that shape. Continue in a similar way by having pupils find and color the shapes that should be yellow, blue, green, or brown.

## Special Populations
*Color-blind children.* You may find a few children in your class who are color-blind or have difficulty distinguishing and naming colors. Try to have these children examined by a school nurse. If any children are color-blind, label crayons and paint, and teach these children to identify the labels. Do not frustrate color-blind children by emphasizing color recognition.

If others have trouble distinguishing and naming colors, give regular practice by using color names (the green book, the yellow chalk, for example).

6

page 6

D'Nealian Handwriting, Book 1. © Scott, Foresman and Company.

31

...sifies objects that belong in a set.
• Marks each object that belongs in a set.
• Uses eye-hand coordination to draw a line between parallel curved lines.

## Teaching

Have pupils turn to page 7. Provide assistance for any students who have difficulty.

Call attention to the first three pictures on the left at the top of the page. Discuss with pupils how all these pictures are alike. If no one brings out the fact that each thing is soft or fuzzy, bring it up yourself. Then ask pupils to listen carefully as you give the following instructions:

—Look at the pictures below. Mark the pictures of objects that are soft and fuzzy.

Then ask pupils to look at the picture of a nurse at the top of the right side of the page. Discuss the picture, pointing out that the nurse is on the phone. Explain that the patient at the bottom of the page has just called the nurse. Then give the following instructions:

—The nurse must go to the patient's house. Help the nurse find the way. Draw a line from the nurse to the patient without touching the edge of the road.

Later evaluate pupils' work on the page to determine those who need reinforcement of the skills represented on the page. You will want to note those students who will benefit from extra activities designed to increase eye-hand coordination or the ability to identify objects that belong in a set.

## Special Populations

Immature pupils, those who cannot focus their vision successfully for close work, and those who have not yet established a sense of left and right or top and bottom will not be able to do Lesson 3 as it is presented on page 7. For those pupils who had difficulty following instructions on pages 5 and 6, use only the left side of page 7 at this time. Save the

name

page 7

right side of the page until the less mature pupils have gained enough skill to handle the maze without frustration. Refer to "Problems in Classroom Learning" in the introduction for a discussion of the reasons why certain pupils cannot succeed with daily assignments.

# Lesson 4, page 8

## Objectives
- Writes number (2–10) that shows how many objects are in a set.
- Uses eye-hand coordination to draw a line from one numbered dot to the next in sequence (0–10).

## Teaching

Help pupils find page 8 in their books. Call attention to the numbers 0–10 at the top of the page. Have pupils trace the numbers with their pencils. Point out the groups of objects below. Say:

–Write the numbers that tell how many objects are in each group.

Tell pupils to count the objects carefully and to use their best handwriting.

Help pupils find the dot-to-dot puzzle at the right side of the page. Point out the number 0 and the dot beside it. Say:

–Put your pencil on the dot beside the number 0. Starting at 0, connect the numbered dots in order to make a picture appear.

You will want to check pupils' responses to be aware of individuals who lack understanding of numbers (0–10) representing objects in a set. Evaluate students' eye-hand coordination and knowledge of sequential order of numbers (0–10) on the dot-to-dot puzzle. Note pupils who will need reinforcement in these areas.

## Special Populations

The pupils who struggled with pages 5, 6, and 7 will need special help to do Lesson 4 on page 8. These children cannot follow oral instructions to find a given place on a page filled with pictures and other details. Do not attempt page 8 with these pupils until they have had considerable practice writing numbers on the chalkboard and on lined writing paper.

As your pupils do Lesson 4, be alert for those who have difficulty connecting the numbered dots in sequence. Use the clown activity to identify pupils who need more practice following number sequence. Keep in mind that several perceptual tasks are involved in following the dots successfully. Frequent changes in the direction of pencil movement must be coordinated with vision, figure/ground interpretation, and sequence of numbers. This activity may be too complex for some pupils in your class.

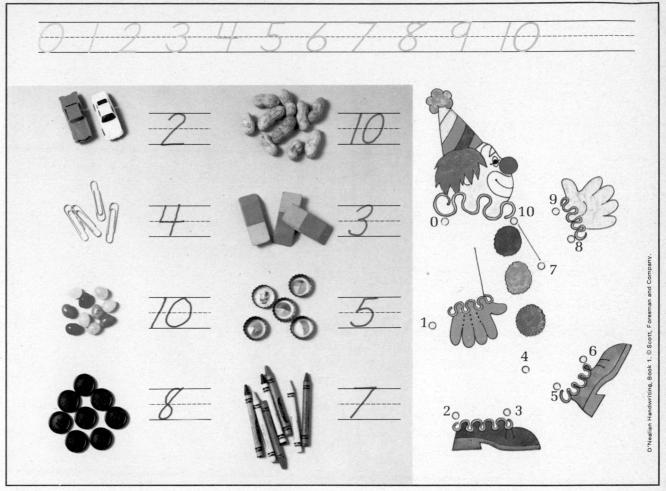

page 8

D'Nealian Handwriting, Book 1. © Scott, Foresman and Company.

# SECTION 2
## pages 9, 10, 11, 12

Lesson 1, page 9 (assessment)
Lesson 2, page 10 (review)
Lesson 3, page 11 (review)
Lesson 4, page 12 (review)

## Lesson 1, page 9

### Objectives
- Develops visual discrimination by matching letters that are identical.
- Marks a letter that matches a cue letter.

### Preparation
*Ahead of time.* Collect or write sets of four letters in which two letters are exactly alike. Be ready to display the letters in a way similar to that in each group on page 9. You may want to use letter combinations such as the following:

d d a o    B D B H
i u i m    N M X N
f h l f    O O Q S

*Class time.* Display the letters you have collected. Have pupils look at the first letter in a group and then find the letter that is exactly like it.

### Teaching
Have pupils turn to page 9. Direct pupils' attention to the left side of the page. If pupils can identify the letters as such, have them do so; if not, do so yourself. Tell pupils to look at the row across the top of the page (it is not necessary for pupils to name the letters) and to find a letter that is exactly like the

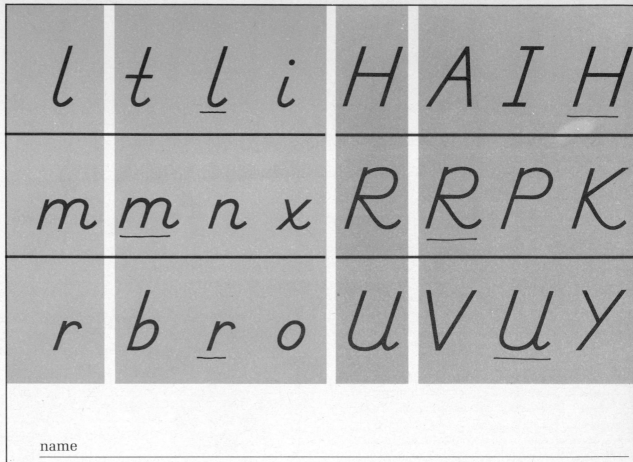

l t l i    H A I H

m m n x    R R P K

r b r o    U V U Y

name _____

page 9

first one. If some do not choose the second letter, help them see why their choice is wrong. Have pupils mark the letters that are the same.

Proceed similarly with each row, making sure that pupils match the shape of the letters.

### Activities
After you have assessed pupils' needs from the responses on the pretests, list the students who need review in the areas covered in the assessment. Then determine which pages or parts of pages in Sections 2 and 3 each group of children should complete.

Students who performed well on any or all of the assessments may participate in the following activities, while pupils needing reinforcement on particular skills are meeting with the teacher and completing the pages in Sections 2 and 3 that meet their needs.

Children's motor skills develop at different rates. It is important that children be allowed to proceed in handwriting at their own rates. Some children will need more time and drill at each stage than others. More mature children should be encouraged to move on as quickly as their abilities allow, since they will have a great sense of accomplishment as they learn to express themselves in writing.

*Size classification.* Give a box of assorted buttons and beads to a group of two or three children. Tell them to work together, sorting the items into sets that are the same size.

*Classification scrapbook.* This activity in classification also develops motor coordination in that it requires children to cut things out with scissors.

Encourage children to make a scrapbook about things that have some characteristic in common. Some suggested topics are blue things, yellow things, things that can go, animals on the farm, things that make noise, things that are tall, or any other topic children dream up.

Individual booklets may be made with colored construction paper for covers and unlined newsprint for the insides. Provide old magazines, catalogs, paste, scissors, pencils, and crayons.

When the scrapbooks are complete, allow children to share them with the class and put them on display in the classroom.

*Macaroni numbers.* Provide pupils with paper, pencils, macaroni, and white glue. Tell them to write a large number on the paper, go over it with glue, and put macaroni on it. Put the numbers on display in the classroom.

*Number scrapbook.* Provide pupils with construction paper, pencils, magazines, scissors, and glue. Tell them to write one number from 0 to 10 at the top of each paper. Instruct pupils to find pictures to show how many each number stands for. Ask them to use objects that are similar on each page. For instance, they may need to find five pictures of a bicycle for the 5 page, six pictures of some kind of cookie for the 6 page, and so on.

*Lotto.* For a small-group activity, make two matching sets of lotto cards. Paste small squares of red, yellow, green, and brown construction paper onto cardboard. On each square, draw a shape pupils know. Have the leader keep one set of cards. Each child gets several cards from the other set. The leader holds up a card and asks for the matching card. For instance, the leader might say, "Who has the red card with a circle on it?" The child who has that card wins the leader's matching card. Play continues until pupils have won all the cards. The pupil with the most cards wins the game.

*Stringing beads.* Have a supply of large wooden or plastic beads on hand and ample shoelaces or other stringing material. Instruct pupils to string the beads, using only one size or only one color. When they finish that, they may then string the beads, using any combination they wish.

*Hidden pictures.* Make worksheets of hidden objects similar to the ones below. Have pupils find a particular object and color it.

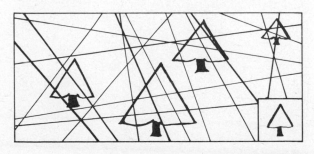

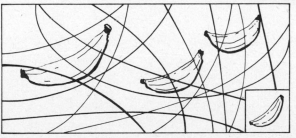

*Puzzles.* If you have some puzzles in the classroom, allow children to spend some time working them. After they have had some experience working these puzzles, let them cut a picture out of a magazine and paste the picture onto a piece of construction paper. Tell children to cut the picture into two or three angled pieces. Let the pupils assemble the pieces back into a picture. Two children can then scramble their picture pieces together and try to reassemble both pictures.

# Lesson 2, page 10

## Objective
- Colors a pictured object to show that it is in the middle of two other objects.

## Preparation
*Ahead of time.* Determine from the results of the assessment on page 5 which children need reinforcement in locational skills (top, middle, bottom). It is possible that some children may not need to work on this page. You may assign pupils who do not need reinforcement in the skill covered on this page to do any of the activities presented at the end of Lesson 1.

Have on hand a crayon for each child.

## Teaching
Have pupils turn to page 10. Identify the pictures as hanging plants, drawers, cups or mugs, ice cream, and blocks.

Ask pupils to look at the hanging plants at the left. Point out the three plants. Explain that there is one plant on top, one in the middle, and one on the bottom. Ask pupils to put their fingers on the top plant. Check the location of pupils' fingers and help any who have selected the incorrect plant. Next, ask pupils to put their fingers on the bottom plant. Make sure pupils have their fingers on the correct plant. Now ask pupils to locate the plant in the middle and mark it with their pencils.

Direct pupils' attention to the pictures on the rest of the page. Have pupils color the middle drawer, the middle cup, the middle scoop of ice cream, and the middle block. Some pupils might be able to finish independently. Circulate among pupils to provide assistance if necessary.

page 10

D'Nealian Handwriting, Book 1. ©Scott, Foresman and Company.

# Lesson 3, page 11

## Objective
• Marks two pictured objects to show that they are the *same*.

## Preparation
*Ahead of time.* Determine from the results of the assessment on page 5 which children need reinforcement in matching like objects. It is possible that some children may not need to work on this page. You may assign pupils who do not need reinforcement in the skill covered on this page to do any of the activities presented at the end of Lesson 1.

## Teaching
Have pupils turn to page 11. Have a volunteer identify the pictures as dolls, blocks, rings, and tents, or do so yourself. Point out that some objects in each set vary in size, shape, or color. Ask pupils to listen carefully as you give the following directions:
—Look at the pictures in the first part of the page. Mark the two pictures that are exactly the same.
Tell pupils to study each group of items and mark the two that are the same. Most pupils will be able to finish independently. Circulate among pupils to provide additional assistance if necessary.

name

page 11

# Lesson 4, page 12

### Objectives
- Develops visual discrimination by matching colors and shapes of objects.
- Colors a shape a specific color.

### Preparation
*Ahead of time.* Have a green, orange, blue, black, and yellow crayon for each child or for a small group of children. Determine from the assessment on page 6 which children need reinforcement in discriminating shapes. It is possible that some children may not need to work on this page. You may assign pupils who do not need reinforcement in the skill covered to do any of the activities presented at the end of Lesson 1.

*Class time.* To review colors, hold up a yellow crayon and let a volunteer tell what color it is. Follow the same procedure with a blue, an orange, a green, and a black crayon.

### Teaching
Have pupils turn to page 12 and look at the first shape at the top of the page. Have a volunteer tell what color it is (green). Then ask pupils to find shapes on the page that are exactly like the green one. Tell pupils that they are to use a green crayon to color everything which is that shape. Continue in a similar way by having pupils find and color the shapes that should be yellow, blue, orange, and black.

### Special Populations
*Color-blind children.* See the Special Populations in Section 1, Lesson 2.

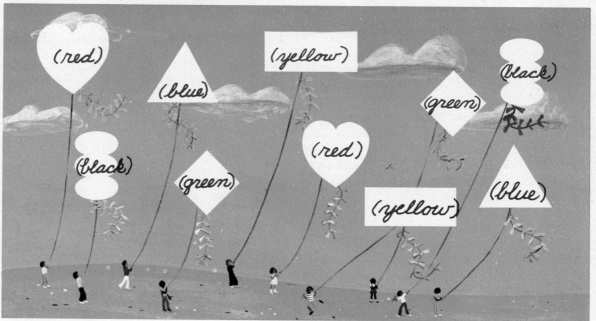

page 12

# SECTION 3
## pages 13, 14, 15, 16

Lesson 1, page 13 (review)
Lesson 2, page 14 (review)
Lesson 3, page 15 (review)
Lesson 4, page 16 (review)

## Lesson 1, page 13 (review)

### Objectives
• Classifies objects that belong in a set.
• Marks each object that belongs in a set.

### Preparation
*Ahead of time*. Review your notes from the assessment on page 7 to determine which children would benefit from reinforcement of classification skills.

Collect several items that are commonly used in the classroom (book, pencil, paper, crayons, chalk, for example) and several items almost never used in a classroom (pan, food, spoon, hat, for example).

*Class time*. Meet with the children you chose to complete this page. Display a few of the school items in a central location. Identify the items with pupils and determine what they might call the set of items (things used in school). Explain that you also have some other items—some of which belong to the same set. Bring out the rest of the items you have collected. Mix up the items related to school with those not related to school, and display them for the group.

Ask students to tell you which items belong with the set of things used in school. If pupils are slow in responding initially, you might identify one item that is often used in school. Have pupils place each item they identify as school-related with the set you started with. If pupils incorrectly classify an object, explain why it doesn't belong with the other items in the set.

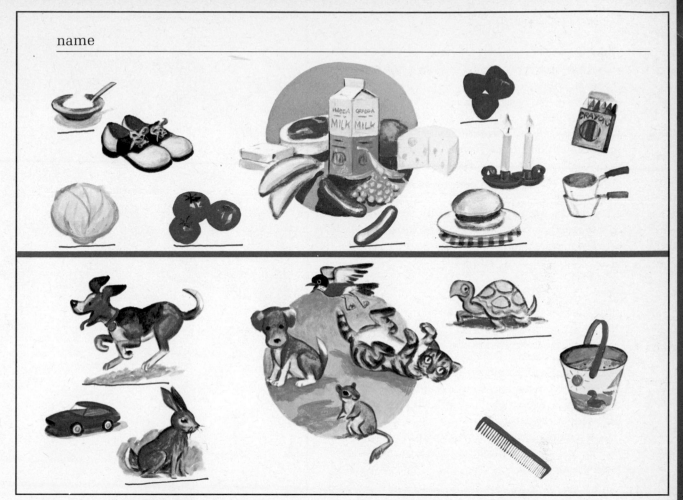

name

page 13

### Teaching
Have pupils turn to page 13. Discuss the set of objects in the circle at the top of the page. Ask pupils what the items in the circle are and what they have in common (food). Point out that other pictures on the top half of the page belong to the same set. Ask a volunteer to identify one picture that also belongs to the food set. Have everyone mark the picture identified by the volunteer. Tell pupils to see how many more pictures they can find and mark that belong to the food set.

When pupils have finished the top half of the page, review the correct answers. Then tell pupils to determine what kind of things are in the next set (animals) and mark pictures that also belong to the set. Let pupils proceed independently. Provide assistance if requested. When everyone has finished, identify the set (live animals) and review the correct answers.

## Lesson 2, page 14

### Objective
- Uses eye-hand coordination to draw a line between parallel lines.

### Preparation
*Ahead of time.* Choose the children that will benefit from additional practice with eye-hand coordination. Children who do not need this practice may be involved in one of the activities at the end of Lesson 1 in Section 2.

Draw some simple paths, similar to the following, on the chalkboard at pupils' eye level. Always indicate the starting point on the left.

*Class time.* Meet at the chalkboard with the group needing reinforcement in eye-hand coordination. Point out the paths on the chalkboard. Instruct each child to draw a line along one path without touching the edges of the path.

Give children plenty of time to practice at the chalkboard. You may want to draw extra paths for more practice.

### Teaching
Have children turn to page 14. Indicate that this page shows several paths a horse may take to get to a lake for a drink. Instruct pupils to start at the beginning and draw a line to show a way the horse can go to get water. Some children may select elaborate paths. Remind them that, however they go, they should not touch the edge of the path.

If children have difficulty staying within the lines, you will want to provide more exercises similar to those covered earlier in this lesson at the chalkboard.

page 14

### Special Populations
Review "Problems in Classroom Learning" in the introduction for symptoms of delayed maturity and poor vision. Page 14 requires mature fine muscle control to mark without touching the edges of the path. For immature children or those with poor vision, begin by holding the child's writing hand as you guide the pupil's finger along the path to the lake. After several rehearsals with the finger, let the child try to mark the same path with a crayon. If this is still too difficult, you should mark the route, then help the pupil trace your marking.

D'Nealian Handwriting, Book 1. © Scott, Foresman and Company.

# Lesson 3, page 15

### Objective
• Writes number (0–10) that shows how many objects are in a set.

### Preparation
*Ahead of time.* Decide which children need additional practice in relating numbers to objects in sets. Refer to the notes you took following the assessment on page 8. Those children who have performed well on the first section of the pretest may participate in one of the activities at the end of Lesson 1 of Section 2.

Have on hand a flannel board and at least ten identical felt shapes.

*Class time.* Meet with children who need practice in using a number to describe how many objects are in a set. To begin the discussion, display a flannel board with nothing on it. Ask a volunteer to write a number on the chalkboard to show how many items are on the flannel board. If no one volunteers, write 0 on the chalkboard yourself. Put one felt shape on the flannel board and ask a volunteer to write the number showing how many forms are on the flannel board.

Continue in this manner until you have ten shapes on the flannel board and the numbers 0–10 are written on the chalkboard.

### Teaching
Help pupils locate page 15 in their books. Point out the numbers at the top of the page. Have pupils trace the numbers with their pencils. Then, instruct pupils to write one of the numbers from the top of the page to show how many leaves are in each picture. Caution pupils to count carefully.

Pupils should be able to complete the page independently. If necessary, guide pupils in identifying the number of leaves in the first picture and writing the number 2 beside it.

page 15

### Special Populations
It is difficult for certain pupils to coordinate vision, speech, hearing, and touch in order to count objects successfully. As your pupils work with page 15, be alert for those who cannot count correctly. Pupils who cannot do page 15 successfully need to work with moveable objects (blocks, large buttons, pieces of chalk) while they practice coordinating vision, speech, hearing, and touch in counting. Provide as much practice as possible to develop sensory coordination for counting.

# Lesson 4, page 16

## Objectives
- Develops visual discrimination by matching letters that are identical.
- Marks a letter that matches a cue letter.
- Writes a sample of handwriting on page 111.

## Preparation
*Ahead of time.* Decide which children need additional practice in matching letters that are the same. Those children who have performed well on the assessment on page 9 may participate in one of the activities at the end of Section 2, Lesson 1.

## Teaching
Have pupils turn to page 16. Provide assistance for any pupils who have difficulty.

Direct pupils' attention to the left side of the page. Tell pupils to look at the row across the top of the page and find a letter that is exactly the same as the first one. It is not necessary for pupils to name the letters. If some children do not choose the second letter, help them see why their choice is wrong. Have pupils mark the letters that are the same.

Proceed similarly with each row, or have pupils work independently by marking the letter that matches the cue letter.

When the group has finished this page, ask the whole class to find page 111 at the end of the book. Provide assistance in finding the page. Follow the instructions for page 111 following Section 30 in this Teacher's Edition.

page 16

D'Nealian Handwriting, Book 1. © Scott, Foresman and Company.

# SECTION 4

## Lesson 1, page 17

### Objectives
- Identifies letter *a* in printed words.
- Traces and writes manuscript letter *a*.
- Draws a line between parallel curved lines.

### Preparation

*Ahead of time.* On the chalkboard, write several words that contain the letter *a* from the children's reading program. If children are not reading yet, you may want to use the activity at the end of this lesson.

Also have on hand examples of lower-case *a*'s that children are likely to see in books. Some examples are shown below:

**a  a  a  *a*  a  a**

*Class time.* Review the words on the board, pointing out the letter *a* in the first word. Ask volunteers to identify the letter *a* in the other words.

Then point out the *a*'s you have collected and tell pupils that books may show different kinds of *a*'s. Write a D'Nealian *a* on the board and explain that this is the kind of *a* children will learn to write.

### Teaching

Instruct students to turn to page 17. When everyone has located the page, read the word *alligator*. Ask pupils to underline the first letter *a* in the word. Demonstrate on the chalkboard. Ask pupils if they see another *a* in the word. Follow the same procedure

alligator          bananas          umbrella

name

page 17

with the other pictures. Point out that *a* is found in different positions in words.

Instruct pupils to find the writing line and look at the parts of the letter *a* as you give the following directions.

—Start at the middle line; go left around, down to the bottom line, around and up to the beginning; close; retrace down, and swing up.

[Around, down, up, down, and a monkey tail.]

Have pupils trace the first *a* following the models as

you give the directions again. Demonstrate on the chalkboard. As pupils trace and write the letter independently, repeat the directions when necessary. Point out that pupils should take particular care in the second row when the starting dot is not provided.

Call attention to the green light near the middle of the page. Instruct pupils to draw a line along the path to the red light without touching the lines.

Give students time to practice making a row of the letter *a* at the bottom of the page.

## Special Populations

For pupils with learning problems (see "Problems in Classroom Learning" in the introduction), mark starting points with color cues. Help them work left to right. Have them finger trace several times before using a pencil. Teach them to say the letter name.

## Activity

*Letter identification.* If children have not yet begun to read and are not familiar with words as such, plan to bring to class objects or pictures of objects that have the letter *a* in their names. Present the names of the objects to pupils, and guide them in identifying the letter *a* within each word.

## Lesson 2, page 18

### Objectives

- Identifies letter *d* in printed words.
- Traces and writes manuscript letter *d* and words that contain *d*.
- Draws a line from one numbered dot to the next in sequence (0–10).

### Preparation

*Ahead of time.* On the chalkboard, write several familiar words from the reading program that contain the letter *d*.

*Class time.* Present the words on the board and guide pupils in locating the letter *d* in each word.

### Teaching

Have pupils turn to page 18 and locate the pictures and labels. Instruct pupils to locate and underline the *d* in each label. Point out that the letter occurs in a different position in each word.

Teach children that the letter *d* begins in the same location as the letter *a*. Write *a* and *d* on the chalkboard and ask pupils what the difference is between the letters.

Instruct pupils to find the writing line beneath the pictures and to look at the parts of the letter *d* as you give these directions:

—Start at the middle line; go left around, down to the bottom line, around up to the top line; retrace down, and swing up.

[Around, down, up high, down, and a monkey tail.]

As pupils practice writing the letter *d*, repeat the directions if necessary.

Direct children to look at the picture and the label *dad*. Identify the letters in the word *dad* and instruct children to trace the word. Tell children to note the amount of space between each letter in the word as they trace. Caution against leaving too much space between letters. Circulate around the room, checking letter spacing as children write.

Tell children to locate the number 0 (zero) in the group of numbers in the right-hand corner. Have them connect the dots beside the numbers in numerical order to see what animal will appear. When pupils have finished, ask what animal their picture resembles.

dinosaur saddle road

dad add

duck

page 18

## Lesson 3, page 19

### Objectives
- Identifies letter *o* in printed words.
- Traces and writes manuscript letter *o* and a word that contains *o*.
- Draws a line from one numbered dot to the next in sequence (0–9).

### Preparation
*Ahead of time.* Have on hand a flannel or magnet board and some felt or paper letters (*a*, *d*, and *o*).
*Class time.* Display the letters. Ask for volunteers to identify the letters *a* and *d*. Then ask if anyone can locate the letter *o*.

### Teaching
Have students turn to page 19. Direct attention to the first line. Ask students to look at the parts of the letter *o* as you give the directions for writing the letter.
—Start at the middle line; go left around, down to the bottom line, around and up to the beginning; close. [Around, down, up, and close.]

Demonstrate the letter on the chalkboard as you repeat the directions. Tell children to trace the letter in their books as you give the directions. Let children continue tracing and writing the letter *o* independently. Repeat the directions if necessary.

Call attention to the picture labeled *odd*. Discuss with children the meaning of *odd* and what is odd about the picture. Have children trace the word *odd*. Then encourage them to write the word independently, paying attention to the spacing between letters.

Direct pupils' attention to the picture of the octopus and the label *octopus*. Ask a volunteer to

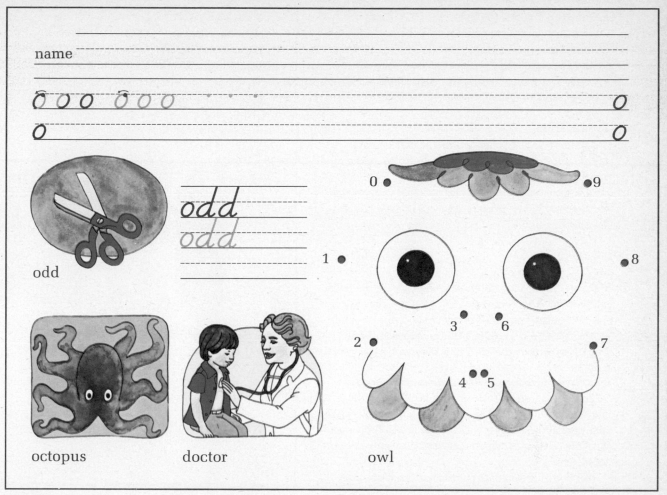

page 19

locate the first letter *o* in the word *octopus*. Have pupils underline it. Then ask if pupils see another letter *o* in the word. Use the same procedure with *doctor*.

Have children locate the number 0 (zero) on the right and connect the numbers in the correct order. Ask children what animal appears when the numbers are connected.

**Special Populations**
Continue teaching eye-hand-voice coordination as

pupils see the letter, trace it, and say its name all at the same time. Put color cues on the work pages of pupils who cannot find the starting point themselves. Watch for backward strokes (clockwise) as pupils write *o* and *d*. "Problems in Classroom Learning" in the introduction) will help you identify pupils who need extra practice and close supervision.

Left-handed pupils may have trouble connecting the dots because their writing hand will cover the dot pattern.

# Lesson 4, page 20

## Objectives
- Identifies letter *g* in printed words.
- Traces and writes manuscript letter *g* and words and phrases that contain *g*.

## Preparation

*Ahead of time*. Select words the children are familiar with that contain the letter *g*. Write the words on the chalkboard.

Also have on hand examples of lower-case *g*'s that children are likely to see in books. Some examples are shown below:

**g** *g* *g* **g** **g**

*Class time*. Guide children in identifying the letter *g* in words. Then point out the *g*'s you have collected and tell pupils that books may show different kinds of *g*'s. Write a D'Nealian *g* on the board and tell pupils that this is the kind of *g* they will learn to write.

## Teaching ▬▬▬▬▬▬

Direct children to turn to page 20. Discuss the pictures at the top of the page, and guide children in identifying the letter *g* within each label. Point out that the letter *g* occurs in different positions in each word.

Tell pupils to look at the parts of the letter *g* on the first writing line as you give the following directions:

—Start at the middle line; go left around, down to the bottom line, around up to the middle line; close; retrace down, and go half a line below the bottom line; hook to the left.

[Around, down, up, down, and a fishhook under water.]

Remind students that *g* has a descender (or tail), which falls below the line. Demonstrate on the chalkboard. Instruct pupils to trace the letter in their books as you reread the directions. Have pupils continue independently, tracing and writing *g*.

a goat     eggs     a flag

go     a dog     a good dog

page 20

Direct children to trace the word *go* under the picture of the traffic light, noting the spacing between letters. Have children look at the words *a dog* as you read them. Point out the spacing between the two words. Have pupils trace the words *a dog* and write them, concentrating on the formation of letters, the spacing between letters, and the spacing between words. Follow the same procedure with the last picture and label.

Give pupils time to practice writing the letter *g*.

## Special Populations

Pupils with learning problems may have trouble with this lesson. Mirror children may confuse the way *d* and *g* should face. Watch for reversals and backward strokes. Provide extra practice to establish correct skills.

## Activity

*Letter hunt*. Supply old magazines and newspapers. Have children cut out words in large print containing the letters *a*, *d*, *o*, and *g*. Then have pupils paste them onto a large piece of paper. This page could then be inserted in a class scrapbook.

D'Nealian Handwriting, Book 1. © Scott, Foresman and Company.

# SECTION 5
## pages 21, 22, 23, 24

Lesson 1, page 21
Lesson 2, page 22
Lesson 3, page 23
Lesson 4, page 24

## Lesson 1, page 21

### Objectives

• Identifies letter *c* in printed words.
• Traces and writes manuscript letter *c* and phrases that contain *c*.
• Draws a line from one numbered dot to the next in sequence (0-9).

### Preparation

*Ahead of time.* Write familiar words containing the letter *c* on the chalkboard. To avoid confusion, use only words in which *c* stands for the k sound. Include a few words that do not have a *c*.

*Class time.* Review the words with children and ask them to find the letter *c* within the words. Ask volunteers to tell you which words do not include that letter.

### Teaching

Have children turn to page 21. Discuss the pictures at the top of the page. Ask students to underline the letter *c* within each label.

Tell students to look at the parts of the letter on the first writing line as you give the following directions:

—Start a little below the middle line; go up to the middle line; go left around, down to the bottom line; curve right and stop.

[Curved start, around, down, up, and stop.]

Direct pupils to begin at the starting dot to trace the letter *c* as you give the directions again. Remind

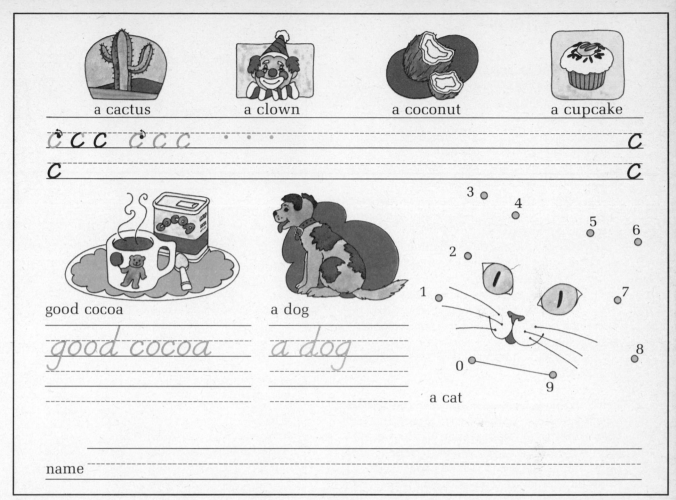

page 21

pupils that the letter *c* begins a little below the middle line. Let students continue independently. Provide assistance where needed.

Discuss the pictures and labels in the middle of the page. Remind children to notice the spacing between words as they trace and write the phrases.

Instruct pupils to locate the number 0 (zero) on the right and draw a line connecting the numbers in order. Ask what appears when the children have finished.

### Special Populations

By now you know which pupils are falling behind in skill development. Those who cannot work fast enough to finish on time may display frustration signals. They constantly erase and have trouble fitting their writing into assigned work space. Require your more frustrated pupils to do only as much writing as they can handle. Reduce the quantity to fit each pupil's ability. Don't require more than a child can do without frustration.

47

# Lesson 2, page 22

## Objectives
- Identifies letter *e* in printed words.
- Traces and writes manuscript letter *e* and words that contain *e*.
- Draws a line between parallel curved lines.

## Preparation

*Ahead of time.* Collect words containing *e* from magazine titles or newspaper headlines.

*Class time.* Write the letter *e* on the chalkboard and name it. Use the oral directions as you demonstrate how to write the letter *e*.

—Start between the middle and bottom lines; curve right up to the middle line; go left around, down to the bottom line; curve right and stop.
[Curve up, around, down, up, and stop.]

Be sure pupils notice the similarities between the letters *c* and *e* (*e* has a small curved line with a *c* wrapped around it).

Display the headlines and titles. Ask a volunteer to find the letter *e*.

## Teaching

Have pupils turn to page 22 and identify the letter on the first line *(e)*. Instruct pupils to look at the parts of the letter *e* as you give the directions again. Let students trace the *e*'s following the models. Allow time for pupils to practice writing the letter *e* independently.

Call attention to the pictures of an elephant and a wheel. Guide children in identifying and underlining the *e*'s in the words beneath the pictures.

Call attention to the pictures. Read the first label. Ask children to trace the two words *a doe*, paying close attention to the amount of space between the two words. Then instruct them to write the two words on their own. Follow the same procedure with the bottom picture.

Ask children to find the man with the shopping cart and to trace his path to the supermarket without touching a line.

page 22

## Activities

*Chalkboard practice.* Give children the opportunity to practice writing the letters *a*, *d*, *o*, *g*, *c*, and *e*, and the words they have learned on the chalkboard. Provide writing lines for them to use while writing the letters they have learned thus far.

*Letter recognition and visual memory.* As children watch, write any one of the following letters on the chalkboard: *a*, *d*, *o*, *g*, *c*, *e*. Quickly erase the letter and ask a volunteer to tell you what letter it was.

Vary the game by writing several or all of the letters at once. Erase one while the children have their eyes closed. Then ask them to tell which letter you erased.

## Lesson 3, page 23

### Objectives
- Identifies letter *s* in printed words.
- Traces and writes manuscript letter *s* and words and phrases that contain *s*.
- Draws a line from one numbered dot to the next in sequence (0–9).

### Preparation
*Class time.* Review the formation of the letters *a*, *d*, *o*, *g*, *c*, and *e*. Have children hold their writing hand in the air and form the letter as you write it on the chalkboard. If necessary, have children practice on paper. Point out that each letter goes around and down to the left.

Explain that the letter *s* begins in the same way as the letter *c*. Write the letter *s* on the chalkboard, giving the following directions:
—Start a little below the middle line; go up to the middle line; go left around, down halfway; then go right around, down to the bottom line; curve left and stop.
[Curved start, around left, and a snake tail.]

### Teaching
Instruct pupils to turn to page 23 and identify the letter on the first line *(s)*. Repeat the directions as pupils follow the steps for making the letter *s*. Have students trace the *s*'s in the first row, using the dots as the beginning points. Allow students plenty of time to practice making the letter independently. Circulate among the children to provide assistance where necessary.

Discuss the pictures and labels. Guide pupils in locating the letter *s* within the labels, and have them underline each one. Ask children which labels contain more than one word. Then ask pupils to explain how they can tell when there is more than one word. (The amount of space between letters is greater.) Instruct children to trace and write the letters in each word, paying close attention to letter formation and spacing.

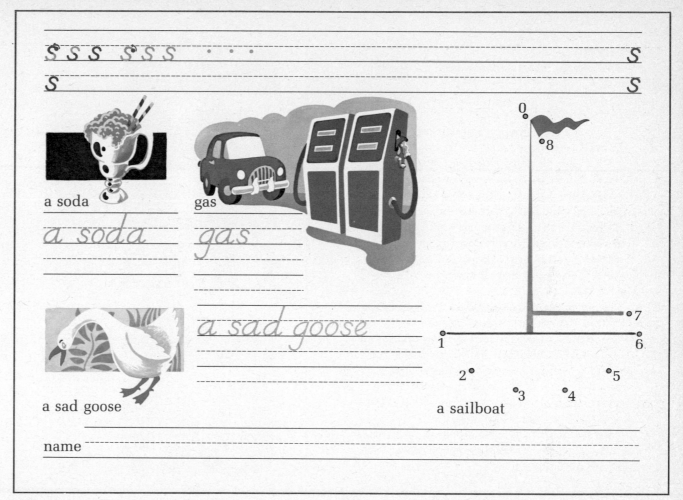

a soda

gas

a sad goose

a sailboat

name

page 23

Call attention to the dot-to-dot puzzle on the right. Ask pupils to start at 0 (zero) and draw a line connecting the numbers in order. When pupils finish, ask them what object appeared when the dots were connected.

### Special Populations
The letter *s* is difficult for dysgraphic and mirror pupils (see "Problems in Classroom Learning" in the introduction). Have these pupils practice on the chalkboard until they know how to change direction in marking *s*. Then give extra practice on one-inch ruled primary writing paper. Watch for frustration, reversed letters, and confusion between *e* and *s*.

Help right-handed pupils turn the page in connecting the dots so their writing hand does not cover the dots.

# Lesson 4, page 24

### Objective
- Traces and writes a noun in both singular and plural forms.

### Preparation
*Ahead of time.* Collect pairs of various items used in the classroom (erasers, pencils, books, and so on).

*Class time.* Hold up one object (for example, a book) and write the name on the chalkboard. Then hold up the matched pair of objects (two books), and write the word *books* beneath *book* on the chalkboard. Ask a volunteer to tell what is different about the second word. After discussing several pairs of objects, explain that we often add *-s* to the end of a word to show that there is more than one.

### Teaching
Have children turn to page 24 and identify the first two pictures. Have them trace the word *cage* and write it independently. Ask students what will be added to the word *cage* when there is more than one cage (*-s*). Explain that in all the words on the page—and in many others like them—we add *-s* to show that they mean more than one.

Permit students to complete the page independently. Provide extra guidance for those who are having difficulty.

### Activity
*Clothespin match.* To increase and reinforce the concept that we add *-s* to some nouns to make them plural, provide activities such as the following in a learning-center environment. Cut a 4-by-12-inch piece of poster board. In a column, print numbers and singular nouns the children are familiar with. A list might look like this:

page 24

Label the correct number of clothespins with the letter *s*. Children will clip the clothespins after the nouns that should be plural, according to the number they are paired with. The card can be made to be self-correcting by providing the letter *s* on the back of the card in the correct positions. Children simply turn the card over to see if they placed the clothespins in the correct positions.

50

# SECTION 6

**pages 25, 26, 27**

Lesson 1, preparation for page 25
Lesson 2, page 25
Lesson 3, page 26
Lesson 4, page 27

## Lesson 1, preparation for page 25

### Objective
• Writes number (0–10) that correctly shows how many objects are in a set.

### Teaching, preparation for page 25

*Ahead of time.* Prepare a worksheet similar to the one shown below. Have one for each child. If you do not have the numbers 0–10 on display in the classroom, write them on the chalkboard.

page 25

*Class time.* Distribute worksheets and have children write their names in the upper left-hand corner. Explain that there are bugs in most of the boxes on the worksheet. Pupils are to count the number of bugs in each box and write that number.

## Lesson 2, page 25

### Objective
• Writes number (0–10) that correctly shows how many objects are in a set.

### Preparation
*Class time.* If necessary, review the formation of the numbers 0–10 on the board.

### Teaching
Instruct children to turn to page 25. If you feel that children need practice writing the numbers 0–10, instruct them to copy the numbers on the blank writing line.

Call attention to the picture of the bags. Explain that each bag contains a different number of objects.

Instruct students to count the objects in each bag and to write the number that shows how many objects there are.

### Special Populations
Provide chalkboard practice and finger tracing of cutout numbers for pupils who reverse or write bottom to top. Help pupils with poor eye-finger-voice coordination count the objects in the bags correctly. Watch for frustration signals.

51

## Activities

*Number formation review.* Allow children extra opportunities to practice the formation of numbers. Use of the chalkboard is especially beneficial because you can easily spot errors and provide guidance.

*Modeling clay and stylus.* Allow children time to practice writing numbers 0–10 with a stylus in a flattened slab of modeling clay. The clay can be placed in an empty handkerchief box or other shallow box. Provide models for children to check so they do not reinforce poor habits. Close teacher supervision is desirable.

## Lesson 3, page 26

### Objectives
- Identifies letter *f* in printed words.
- Traces and writes manuscript letter *f* and words and phrases that contain *f*.

### Preparation
*Ahead of time.* Select familiar vocabulary words containing the letter *f* from the children's reading program. Display the words on flash cards or on the chalkboard.

*Class time.* Guide children in identifying the letter *f* within each word.

### Teaching ▄▄▄▄▄▄▄

Have children turn to page 26. Discuss and identify the pictures at the top of the page. Guide children in locating and underlining the letter *f* in each label.

Call attention to the models of the letter *f* on the first writing line. Point out that this letter begins like *c* and *s*, except that it begins near the top line. Have children look at the models as you give the directions for forming the letter.

—Start a little below the top line; go up to the top line; go left around, slant down to the bottom line. Make a crossbar on the middle line.

[Curved high start, around, down. Cross.]

page 26

As you repeat the directions, instruct pupils to trace the three *f*'s. Remind pupils to begin at the starting dot near the top line. Have pupils complete the row of *f*'s.

Call attention to and discuss the pictures and labels on the bottom half of the page. Ask which labels have more than one word [*a safe, a face, a sad face*]. Have children trace and write the labels, paying close attention to the starting position of the letter *f* and the spacing between letters and words. Most pupils will be able to finish the page independently.

### Activity

*Letter puzzles.* Instruct pupils to write on construction paper all the letters they have learned so far [*a, d, o, g, c, e, s,* and *f*]. Demonstrate on the chalkboard that the letters should be scattered on the

52

paper. Emphasize that children should write very large. Have pupils cut their papers into pieces to make puzzles. Later, children may put the puzzles together again.

## Lesson 4, page 27

### Objectives
- Identifies letter *b* in printed words.
- Traces and writes manuscript letter *b* and words and phrases that contain *b*.
- Draws a line between parallel curved lines.

### Preparation
*Ahead of time.* Collect magazine or newspaper headlines containing the letter *b*.

*Class time.* Write the letter *b* on the chalkboard, giving the following directions at the same time:
—Start at the top line; slant down to the bottom line; go right around, up to the middle line; curve left and close.
[ High start, down, around, up into a tummy. ]

Display the headlines and ask for volunteers to identify the letter *b*.

### Teaching

Have pupils turn to page 27 and identify the letter on the first line *(b)*. Repeat the directions as pupils look at the models showing the parts of the letter on the first line. Have students trace the *b*'s in the first line, using the starting dot as the beginning point. Allow students time to practice making the letter independently. Circulate among children to provide assistance where necessary.

Discuss the pictures and their labels. Ask children which labels contain more than one word. If necessary, review how they can tell when there is more than one word. (The amount of space between letters is greater.) Instruct children to trace and write the letters in each word.

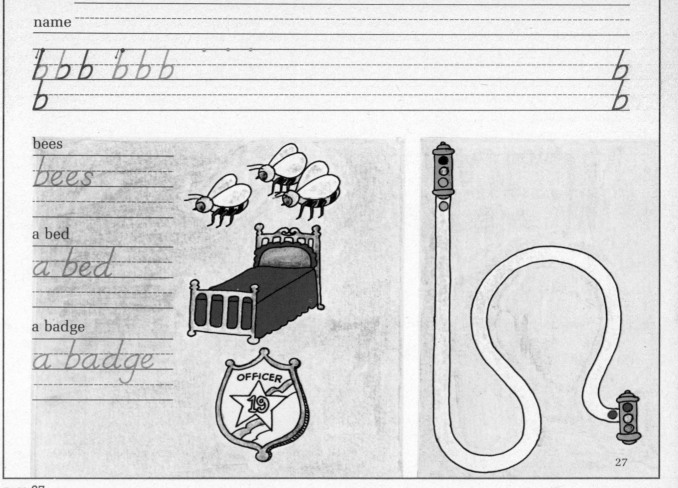

page 27

Tell children to place their pencil points on the green light to the right. Then have them trace the path to the red light without touching a line.

### Activity
*Letter game.* Display the letters *a, d, o, g, c, e, f,* and *b* on the chalkboard. The leader begins the game by saying "I'm thinking of a letter, and it . . . ." The leader then gives a clue, such as "has a tail that hangs below the bottom line." Players take turns guessing which letter it is. The leader gives more clues if necessary. The person who guesses the correct letter is the next leader.

# SECTION 7

pages 28, 29, 30

Lesson 1, page 28
Lesson 2, page 29
Lesson 3, preparation for page 30
Lesson 4, page 30

## Lesson 1, page 28

### Objectives
• Identifies letter *l* in printed words.
• Traces and writes manuscript letter *l* and phrases that contain *l*.

### Preparation
*Ahead of time*. Choose several vocabulary words containing the letter *l* that children have been exposed to in their reading program. Plan to display the words on the chalkboard.

*Class time*. Assist children in identifying the letter *l* within the first word. Point out that this letter is one of the thinnest letters in the alphabet and is tall like the letter *f*. Demonstrate the letter on the chalkboard while giving the following directions:

—Start at the top line; slant down to the bottom line, and swing up.

[ High start, down, and a monkey tail. ]

Ask volunteers to identify the letter *l* in the rest of the vocabulary words.

### Teaching

Instruct pupils to turn to page 28 and identify the letter at the top of the page *(l)*. Ask pupils to look at the first letters on the left as you give the directions again. Remind students to start at the top line as they trace and write the letter *l* on the writing lines at the top of the page.

Discuss the pictures and their labels with students. Emphasize formation of *l* as pupils trace and write the words independently.

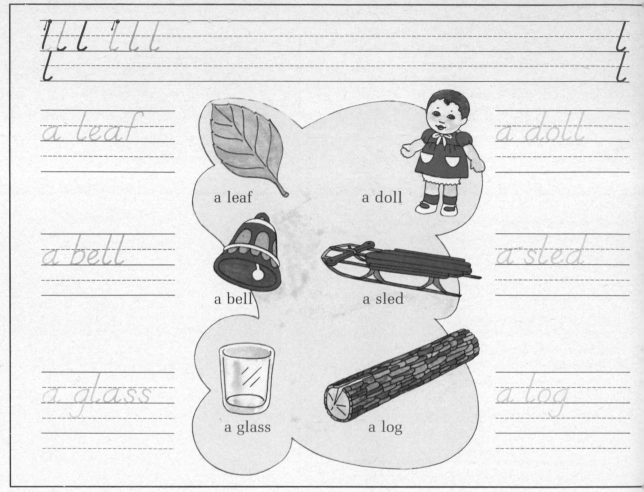

a leaf

a bell

a glass

a doll

a sled

a log

page 28

## Lesson 2, page 29

### Objectives
• Identifies letter *t* in printed words
• Traces and writes manuscript letter *t* and words and phrases that contain *t*.

### Preparation
*Class time*. Write the letter *l* on the board as you review its formation. Indicate that the letter *l* is similar to *t*. Demonstrate this by writing the first step of the letter *t*, and comparing it to the letter *l* on the board. Then complete the letter *t*, using the following directions:

—Start at the top line; slant down to the bottom line, and swing up. Make a crossbar on the middle line.

[ High start, down, and a monkey tail. Cross. ]

Compare the letters *t* and *l*. Ask a volunteer to tell you what the difference is between the letters (the cross bar at the middle line on the letter *t*).

## Teaching

Have pupils turn to page 29 and discuss the pictures at the top of the page. Guide pupils in identifying the letter *t* within the words below the pictures. Ask pupils to identify the letter on the first line *(t)*. Repeat the directions for writing *t* as pupils look at the letter models. Have pupils trace three *t*'s, use the dots for starting points, and write three or more *t*'s independently.

Have the pictures identified. Ask pupils which of the labels include more than one word *(a belt, a taco, a fat toad)*. Review how they will show that there is more than one word. (They will allow more space between words.) Instruct pupils to trace and write the words next to the pictures. Circulate among pupils to provide help where needed.

## Activity

*Letter identification game.* Write all the letters children have learned thus far *(a, d, o, g, c, e, s, f, b, l, and t)* on the chalkboard. Then write the beginning step of any one of the letters. Ask pupils if they can tell you which letter you are forming. If no one can, provide the next step, and so on. When someone provides the correct letter, complete the letter so everyone can see.

# Lesson 3, preparation for page 30

## Objectives
- Demonstrates ability to follow instructions by relating colors with responses.
- Identifies plural nouns when heard.
- Writes a noun and adds *-s* to form a plural.

## Teaching, preparation for page 30

*Ahead of time.* Cut cards from red and green construction paper to measure about 3- by 5-inches. Provide enough cards so that each child will have one red and one green card. Children will use these cards to signal responses during class.

a tiger        mittens        a rabbit

a belt        a taco

bat        a fat toad

name

page 29

Have on hand several identical small objects (pencils, for example).

*Class time.* Distribute one green card and one red card to each child. Explain that you are going to ask them to hold up the green card when you say words that mean there is more than one. Have pupils write 2–10 on the green card. Remind pupils that we often add *-s* to words that mean more than one. Tell them to hold up the red card when they hear you say words that stand for only one thing. Have them write

number 1 on the red card.

Demonstrate by holding up one pencil and saying *one pencil.* Indicate that children should hold up the red card because there is only one pencil. Now hold up two pencils and say *two pencils.* Ask a volunteer to tell which card children should hold up (green card). Continue in this manner with convenient classroom objects until you are sure everyone understands the procedure. The number acts as an extra clue, so be sure to also emphasize the letter *s* at the end of the word. Explain that later you will not hold up objects.

Begin the exercise by using a number and any familiar nouns. For instance, you might say *one bed* and give children time to hold up their red cards. Then you might say *five dolls* and wait for children to respond by holding up their green cards. Continue in this manner, mixing up words, singular and plural forms, and numbers used before plural forms. Try to use all numbers from one through ten.

When children have had sufficient practice identifying singular and plural forms of spoken words, write *1 bed* on the chalkboard and read it. Then write *4 bed*, read it, and ask pupils what you must do to make the word *bed* mean more than one (add *-s*). Let a volunteer come to the board and write *4 beds*. Continue in this manner, using the words *bed, dad, dog, cat, doll, egg, log, bell, soda,* and *sled*.

### Activity

*Chalkboard or worksheet activity.* If you feel that children are able to copy from the board, you may ask them to do the following activity on lined paper. If not, prepare a worksheet similar to the following:

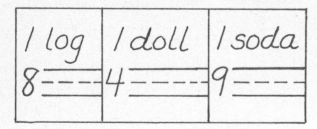

Have pupils write *1 log* (if from chalkboard) and beneath it *8*. Allow them time to complete the plural form of the word on their own.

## Lesson 4, page 30

### Objective
• Writes a noun and adds *-s* to form the plural

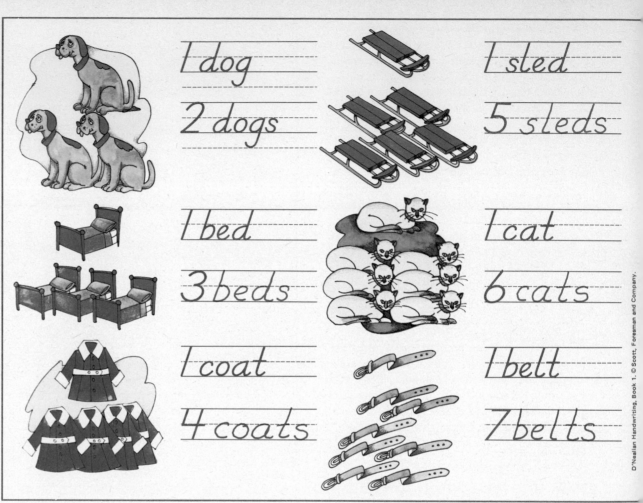

page 30

### Teaching

Have pupils turn to page 30 and identify the first pictures on the left. Explain that the numbers and words describe the pictures. Discuss the pictures and labels, asking:
—How many dogs are in the first picture? [1] in the second picture? [2]
—What is added to the word *dog* to show there is more than one? [-s]

Remind pupils that we often add *-s* to words to show that they mean more than one.

Call attention to the pictures of beds. Discuss the pictures and determine with children which picture shows more than one bed. Tell children to write the word that shows there is more than one bed. Ask a volunteer to explain what was added to the word *bed* to make it mean more than one. (-s)

Children should be able to complete the page independently. Provide assistance for anyone who needs it.

# SECTION 8

**pages 31, 32, 33, 34**

## Lesson 1, page 31

### Objectives
- Identifies letter *h* in printed words.
- Traces and writes manuscript letter *h* and words and phrases that contain *h*.

### Preparation
*Ahead of time.* Select several words containing the letter *h* from the children's reading program. Plan to display the words either on the chalkboard or on flash cards.

*Class time.* Review the words with pupils and guide them in locating the *h* within each word.

### Teaching

Have pupils turn to page 31 and locate the picture of a helicopter. Ask pupils to locate and underline the letter *h* in the word *helicopter.* Identify the next two pictures (a birdhouse and a brush) and their labels. Instruct pupils to underline the letter *h* in each word. Ask students to notice the position of the *h* in each word. It can appear at the beginning, in the middle, and at the end of words.

Call attention to the models of the letter *h* on the writing lines. Point out that the letter *h* begins at the top line, like the letters *l* and *t.* Instruct pupils to look at the parts of the letter *h* while you give the following directions:

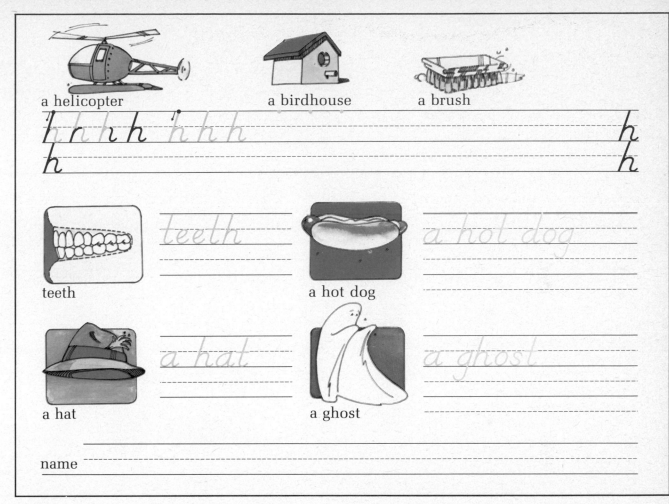

a helicopter      a birdhouse      a brush

teeth

a hot dog

a hat

a ghost

name

page 31

—Start at the top line; slant down to the bottom line; retrace up halfway; make a hump to the right, and swing up.
[High start, down, up, and a hump with a monkey tail.]
Allow time for pupils to trace and write *h.*

Have the pictures identified (teeth, a hat, a hot dog, a ghost). Tell pupils that the word or words beside each picture describe it. Point out that three of the pictures have more than one word beside it. Caution students to leave more space between words. Have pupils trace and write the words.

57

## Lesson 2, page 32

### Objectives
- Identifies letter *k* in printed words.
- Traces and writes manuscript letter *k* and words and phrases that contain *k*.

### Preparation
*Ahead of time.* Collect words containing *k* from magazine titles or newspaper headlines.
*Class time.* Display the headlines and titles. Guide pupils in identifying the letter *k*.

### Teaching
Instruct children to turn to page 32. Identify the pictures and labels at the top of the page. Guide pupils in locating and underlining the letter *k* in each word.

Indicate that the letter *k* begins very much like the letter *h*. Call attention to the models of the letter *k* on the writing lines. Ask pupils to examine them as you give the following directions:
—Start at the top line; slant down to the bottom line; retrace up halfway; make a loop to the right and close; slant right to the bottom line, and swing up. [High start, down, up, small tummy, and a monkey tail.]

Identify the pictures on the bottom half of the page. Ask pupils which pictures are described by more than one word (a clock, black socks). Ask for volunteers to tell how we show there is more than one word (leave more space between words).

Instruct pupils to trace and write the words next to the pictures, paying close attention to the formation of the new letter *k* and to the spacing between words.

a lake    a block    a koala

a clock    books

black socks

page 32

## Lesson 3, page 33

### Objectives
- Classifies objects that belong in a set.
- Writes the word *hot* or *cold* to describe a pictured object.

### Preparation
*Ahead of time.* Have on hand ice cubes, a cup of cold water or soda, and a cup of warm water, or collect pictures of hot and cold items.
*Class time.* Allow small groups of children to touch the various objects and tell whether each is hot or cold. If you use pictures, ask pupils to imagine how the objects would feel to touch. Encourage pupils to name objects that are cold and those that are hot.

D'Nealian Handwriting, Book 1. © Scott, Foresman and Company.

## Teaching

Have pupils turn to page 33 and identify the letters at the top of the page (c, d, h, l, o, t). If pupils cannot readily identify the letters, do so yourself.

Direct pupils' attention to the first group of objects and identify them (sun, fire, cup of soup). Ask pupils why they think all these objects are grouped together and what is the same about all of them. Call attention to the word hot. Tell pupils that the word hot describes all the pictures in the first box. Let pupils write the word *hot* on the line. Remind pupils that models for all the letters they will need are at the top of the page. Check pupils' work carefully since their writing becomes a model for the rest of the page.

Then have pupils look at the second group of objects and identify them (snow, ice cubes, ice-cream cone). Ask pupils to tell what the pictures have in common. Call attention to the printed word *cold,* and tell pupils that it describes the objects in the second group. Instruct pupils to write the word *cold* on the line. Check their work.

Then direct pupils' attention to the two columns on the bottom half of the page. Tell pupils to write the word *hot* beside each object that is hot and *cold* beside each object that is cold. Some pupils may need item-by-item guidance.

## Special Populations

By now you have identified the pupils who are still confused by directionality, cannot stay within the lines, use backward writing strokes, and cannot keep up with the class. These children need extra practice at the chalkboard and with cutout letters and numbers. They need much multi-sensory drill to develop coordination of seeing, saying, hearing, and touching. When you can, do small-group work in which these pupils practice counting, putting letters and numbers in sequence, working left to right, and writing top to bottom.

page 33

## Activities

*Hot and cold.* Supply pupils with old magazines, scissors, paste, and some construction paper. Pupils can cut out pictures and classify them into sets of hot and cold objects. The pictures may be pasted on construction paper and labeled.

*Collage.* Some pupils may wish to make a collage. Explain, for instance, that they can draw or cut out the letters that spell hot. Then they can cut out pictures of things that can be hot. To make a collage, pupils should overlap the pictures and letters and paste them at different angles.

# Lesson 4, page 34

### Objectives
- Uses visual discrimination to find objects hidden in a picture.
- Writes appropriate label below a pictured object.

### Preparation
*Ahead of time.* Have on hand large pictures that show scenes or several objects.

*Class time.* Show one of the large pictures and ask pupils to point out different details. If children miss an important detail, describe it and ask if they can find it.

### Teaching
Have pupils turn to page 34. Let a volunteer identify the pictures at the top of the page (hat, cake, bell, clock, shoes). Tell pupils to look at the words below the first picture. Ask:

—What is the name of the picture? [hat]

Make sure that pupils relate the words to the pictures above them.

Direct attention to the large picture on the page. Tell them that the same pictures they see at the top of the page are hidden here. Have pupils look at the top row again and point to the picture of the hat. Now ask pupils to look at the large picture and find the picture of the hat. When most pupils have found it, tell them to write the word *hat*. Help others locate the hidden picture and write the word.

Give oral directions for any pupils who do not remember how to form each letter. Some pupils may finish the page independently; others will need guidance for every picture.

### Activity
*Visual discrimination.* On heavy paper, provide a pattern of geometric shapes in blue, yellow, red, and green. The pattern should be similar to the one shown.

page 34

Cover the pattern with clear acetate, or laminate it. On small cards, provide the shapes that belong in the blank squares (yellow square; red circle, square, and parallelogram; blue triangle and parallelogram; green square and parallelogram). Children will use visual discrimination of colors and shapes to place the cards in the correct squares.

# SECTION 9

pages 35, 36, 37, 38

## Lesson 1, page 35

### Objectives
- Identifies letter *i* in printed words.
- Traces and writes manuscript letter *i* and words that contain *i*.
- Classifies pictured objects by size (big and little).

### Preparation
*Ahead of time.* Select several popular children's books (perhaps some you have read to the class) that contain the letter *i* in the title.

*Class time.* Display a book and ask for volunteers to identify the letter *i* in the title. Use the other book titles in the same manner.

### Teaching ■
Have children turn to page 35 and locate the letters on the first writing line. As pupils look at these models, give the directions for forming the letter:

—Start at the middle line; slant down to the bottom line, and swing up. Make a dot above the letter. [Down, and a monkey tail. Add a dot.]

Repeat the directions as pupils trace and write *i*'s on the writing lines. Point out that this is the first letter they have had that has a dot.

Discuss the pictures of elephants and the labels beneath them. Guide children in locating the letter *i* in each label and have them underline it. After discussing the differences between the big and the little elephants, ask children to mention some other animals or objects

page 35

that they think of as big. Then ask them to describe some animals or objects they think of as little.

Call attention to the writing lines next to the picture of the big elephant. Direct children to trace the letters in the word *big*, and then write the word independently. Follow the same procedure with the word *little*.

Call attention to the pictures in the bottom half of the page. Discuss each picture with pupils. Ask pupils to write *big* next to pictures they would describe as big, and *little* next to pictures they would describe as little. Evaluate the sizes of the object in each picture when pupils have finished.

## Lesson 2, page 36

### Objectives
- Identifies letter *u* in printed words.
- Traces and writes manuscript letter *u* and words that contain *u*.
- Writes appropriate label beside picture.

### Preparation

*Ahead of time.* Bring to class some pictures of familiar animals or objects that have names containing the letter *u* (puppy, bus, lunch, and so on). Write the names on the chalkboard. Underline the letter *u* in the first word.

*Class time.* Display each picture while simultaneously introducing the word. Point out the underlined *u* in the first word, and ask volunteers to locate the letter *u* in the other words you introduce. Underline the *u*'s as you proceed.

### Teaching

Have pupils turn to page 36 and identify the letter on the first line *(u)*. Direct pupils to study the model letters while you give the following directions:
—Start at the middle line; slant down to the bottom line; curve right; slant up to the middle line; retrace down, and swing up.
[Down, over, up, down, and a monkey tail.]

Repeat the directions as pupils trace the letter *u* on the writing line following the models. As pupils practice writing the letter *u* independently, repeat directions if necessary.

Call attention to the words at the left. Identify each word and have pupils trace it. Explain that these words are the names of the pictures on the page. However, the pictures are mixed up. Discuss each picture and label with the class. Then have pupils use the words they traced as models and write the labels next to the correct picture.

Have pupils look at the word with number 1 next to it and find the writing line labeled 1. Ask children if the word they traced is the same as the label for

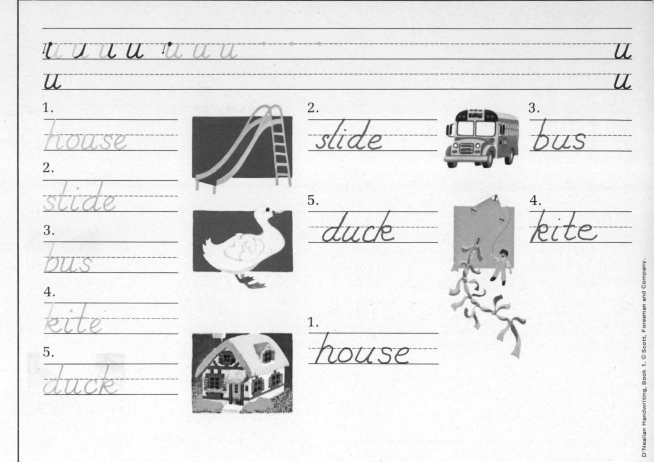

page 36

that picture. Point out that the first word they traced was *house* and that the picture and label indicate a house. Instruct pupils to study the letters they traced in the word *house* and to write the word next to the picture of the house.

Most pupils can continue independently. Provide assistance where necessary.

### Activity

*Letter reinforcement.* Use a felt-tip pen to write on cardboard a large model of a manuscript letter, including directional arrows and beginning dot. Cover the cardboard with clear acetate, or laminate it. Children may trace the letters using crayons.

D'Nealian Handwriting, Book 1. © Scott, Foresman and Company.

## Lesson 3, page 37

**Objectives**
- Identifies letter *w* in printed words.
- Traces and writes manuscript letter *w* and phrases that contain *w*.

**Preparation**

*Ahead of time.* Bring cereal boxes that have the letter *w* in rather large print on the boxes.

*Class time.* Hold up one cereal box and choose a word containing the letter *w* from it. Write the word on the chalkboard and underline the letter *w*. Distribute the cereal boxes to groups of children. Let them look for more words containing the letter *w* on their cereal boxes. Circulate among groups, noting the words children are locating. After a few minutes, write the words on the chalkboard and let children point out the *w*'s.

**Teaching** ▬▬▬▬▬▬

Have children turn to page 37 and identify the pictures at the top of the page. Guide pupils in locating and underlining the letter *w* within the labels for these pictures.

Call attention to the writing lines and give the directions for forming the letter *w* as children study the steps.

—Start at the middle line; slant down to the bottom line; curve right; slant up to the middle line; retrace down; curve right; slant up to the middle line. [Down, over, up, down, over, up.]

As pupils trace and write the letter *w*, repeat the directions when necessary.

Discuss the pictures and labels below the writing lines. Point out that each label has more than one word. Tell children to concentrate on the spacing between letters and words, as well as on the formation of the new letter *w*.

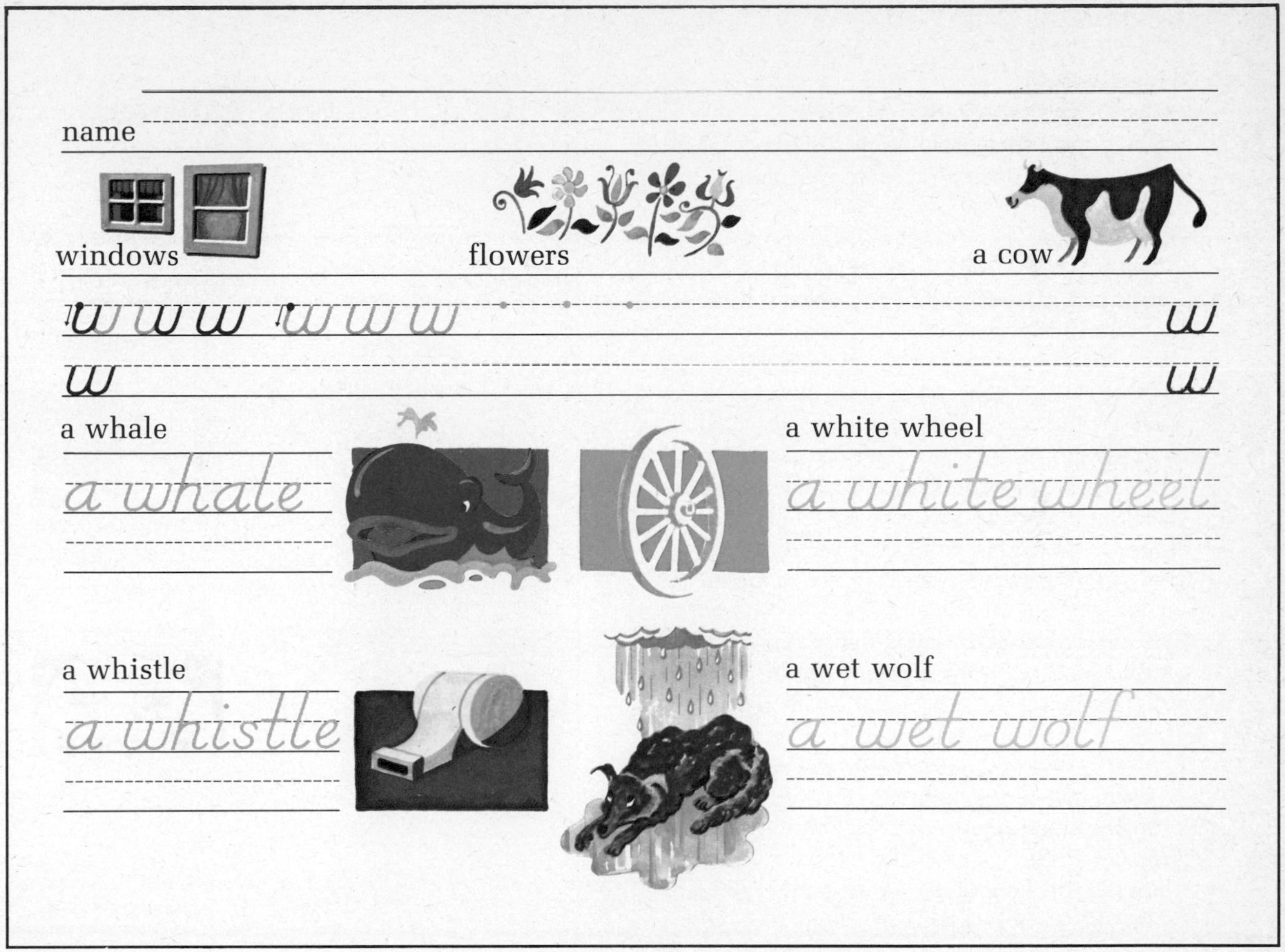

name

windows          flowers          a cow

w w w   w w w                          w
w                                      w

a whale          a white wheel
*a whale*        *a white wheel*

a whistle        a wet wolf
*a whistle*      *a wet wolf*

page 37

# Lesson 4, page 38

## Objectives
- Classifies objects that belong in a set.
- Writes appropriate label below a picture.
- Writes a noun and adds -s to form a plural.

## Preparation

*Ahead of time.* Have on hand several kinds of balls (tennis ball, softball, and so on) and any commercial or teacher-made games.

*Class time.* Mix up the balls and games. Identify and discuss each item. Then ask volunteers to put the objects in two groups that seem to belong together.

If children have trouble grouping the balls and games, help them get started by putting two balls together. See if they can pick it up from there. Give volunteers time to finish grouping the items.

Point out that even though the balls different from each other, they have certain things in common, and they are all balls. Make the same type of observation about the games.

## Teaching

Have pupils turn to page 38. Identify and discuss with pupils the pictures and labels at the top of the page.

For the first item (doll) ask what other types of dolls there might be besides this kind. Students might notice the other dolls on the shelf below. If so, acknowledge that it is another type of doll, and the one on top could be grouped with that one. Ask children what they will need to do to write a label for the picture of three dolls (add the letter -s).

Instruct pupils to write the word *dolls* below the dolls on the shelf. Make sure everyone has the right location and understands the procedure.

Next, direct attention to the picture of the blocks and continue in a similar way.

If necessary, continue in this manner with the last three items. Tell students to use their best handwriting.

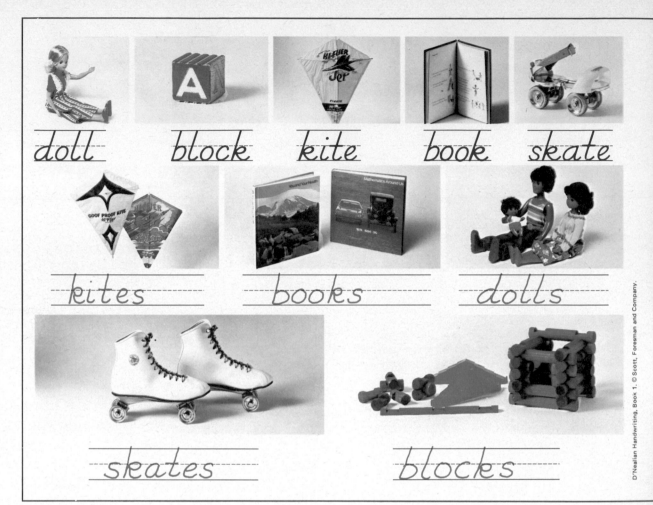

page 38

## Activity

Make flash cards with labeled magazine pictures on one side. Write the plural form of the word on the other side. One pupil starts by laying a card down, picture side up. The next player must tell what the plural form of the word/picture is and write the word on a sheet of paper. If the player can tell what the plural form is, he or she may keep the card.

# SECTION 10

pages 39, 40, 41

## Lesson 1, page 39

### Objectives
• Identifies letter *y* in printed words.
• Traces and writes manuscript letter *y* and phrases that contain *y*.

### Preparation
*Ahead of time.* Write familiar words containing the letter *y* on the chalkboard.

*Class time.* Guide children in identifying the letter *y* within the words. If no one can locate *y* in the first word, underline it.

### Teaching
Have children turn to page 39 and locate the pictures at the top of the page. Identify and discuss the pictures and labels with pupils. Guide pupils in locating and underlining the letter *y* in the labels. Point out that the letter *y* may be found at the beginning, in the middle, or at the end of words.

Call attention to the writing lines with the models of the letter *y*. Give the following directions as pupils study the parts of *y*:

–Start at the middle line; slant down to the bottom line; curve right; slant up to the middle line; retrace down, and go half a line below the bottom line; hook to the left.
[Down, over, up, down under water, and a fish-hook.]

page 39

Emphasize that the letter *y* has a descender (or tail) that hangs down below the bottom line. Ask pupils what other letter they have learned also has a tail that hangs below the line *(g)*.

Repeat the directions as pupils begin to trace the *y*'s following the models. Give assistance where necessary.

Direct pupils' attention to the pictures near the middle of the page. Identify each picture and label, pointing out that each label has more than one word. Review the fact that extra space is needed to show the separation between words. Ask pupils to tell how many words are in each label. Remind pupils to notice the spacing between words and the formation of the new letter *y* as they trace each label and copy the label on the writing line.

If pupils still need practice on the letter *y*, instruct them to practice writing the letter on the writing line at the bottom of the page. Explain that they should try to make their *y*'s look just like the first one on the line.

## Lesson 2, page 40

### Objectives
- Identifies letter *j* in printed words.
- Traces and writes manuscript letter *j* and words and phrases that contain *j*.

### Preparation
*Ahead of time.* Have on hand magazine titles or newspaper headlines that have words with the letter *j* in them.

*Class time.* Display the headlines or titles and ask volunteers to locate the letter *j* within words. You might write the words on the chalkboard and underline the letter *j* in each one.

### Teaching

Have children turn to page 40 and locate the pictures at the top of the page. Identify the pictures and labels. Then ask children to find and underline the letter *j* within the printed labels.

Call attention to the writing line with the models of the letter *j*. Ask pupils to study the parts of the letter as you give the following directions:

—Start at the middle line; slant down half a line below the bottom line; hook to the left. Make a dot above the letter.

[Down, and a fishhook under water. Add a dot.]

Point out that this letter also has a tail that hangs below the line. Remind pupils that they also know another letter that has a dot *(i)*.

Repeat the directions as pupils begin to trace and write the letter *j*. Let pupils continue independently. Provide assistance where necessary.

Discuss the pictures near the middle of the page. Identify each printed label and have pupils trace the manuscript labels. Instruct them to also write each label below the one they traced.

Allow pupils to practice writing the letter *j*. Remind them not to forget the second step of the letter—the dot.

jeans

pajamas

a blue jay

jacks

jelly

a jacket

page 40

# Lesson 3, preparation for page 41

## Objectives

- Draws four pictures showing pupil's own actions before coming to school that day.
- Labels four pictures with 1, 2, 3, and 4 to show sequential order.

## Teaching, preparation for page 41

*Ahead of time.* Have on hand a piece of 9- by-12-inch newsprint for each pupil. If children don't have crayons, be prepared to supply some.

*Class time.* Distribute paper (and crayons, if necessary).

Begin by asking students what things they did that morning from the time they got up until the time they got to school. Most pupils will gladly share details of their experiences that morning. If some children have difficulty recalling what they did, ask questions similar to the following:

—Did you eat breakfast?

—Did you ride the bus or walk to school?

—Who did you see on the way to school?

After pupils share experiences, explain that they are going to draw pictures of four things they did that morning. Tell children to fold the paper in half and then fold it in half again. Demonstrate this with a piece of paper. When they unfold it, the paper will be divided into fourths. Have pupils draw a line along each fold.

Then instruct pupils to draw four pictures of things they did that morning, one in each square. Encourage children to include details. For instance, if they ate breakfast in the kitchen, ask them to show some of the things in the kitchen and other members of the family that were there.

Guide children in labeling their pictures by telling them to put the number 1 by the picture showing what happened first that morning. Continue in this manner with the labeling of each picture.

## Activities

*Cartoon sequence.* Choose several simple comic strips from the newspaper. Mount them on heavy paper, laminate them or cover them with acetate, and cut them apart. Ask children to number the frames of the cartoon to show the order in which they think the action occurred.

*Photo sequences.* If you have a camera, you may want to take photographs of class members working on simple sequential activities (drawing, for example). Then, when the photographs are developed, ask children to put the photos of themselves in order to show the sequence in which they did things.

# Lesson 4, page 41

## Objective

- Writes the number 1, 2, or 3 below each picture in a set of three to show sequence.

## Teaching ▪▬▬▬▬▬

Have pupils turn to page 41. Discuss the pictures of a child drawing at the top of the page. Indicate that all three pictures show the same child at different stages of drawing a picture. Ask children which picture shows the child just starting to draw (middle). Explain that since the middle picture shows the first step of the child drawing, they should label it with the number 1. Have children trace the number 1 below the picture. Then ask which of the other two pictures shows what happened next (last picture). Explain that since this is the second thing that happened, they should label it with the number 2. Then have them trace it. Point to the remaining picture and ask if that shows the third thing that happened (yes). Have pupils trace the number 3. Review the three pictures with pupils, explaining that they have just numbered them in the order in which the stages happened.

Direct attention to the three pictures of the ice-cream cone in the middle of the page. Explain that these pictures are mixed up. Tell pupils to think about the order in which the stages really happened, while the person ate the ice-cream cone. Instruct them to label each picture with the number 1, 2, or 3 to show which stage happened first, second, or third. Tell pupils to concentrate on writing the numbers like the models they traced near the last pictures. Most children will be able to complete the page independently. However, be prepared to provide guidance similar to that used with the top row of pictures with any pupils who are unsure of their responses.

## Special Populations

Perceiving information or action in sequence is difficult for pupils with learning problems, yet it is an important skill in handwriting. Mirror-oriented children perceive sequence right to left, or partly so. Pupils with poor visual memory often scramble the sequence. They do not notice the clues that show cause-effect relationships or what must happen before the next step can take place.

This lesson will reveal which pupils must have more practice and individual help with sequence. For these children, incorporate the concept of sequence into as many daily activities as possible. Gradually these less mature pupils will begin to understand the concept of step-by-step sequence.

page 41

# SECTION 11
## pages 42, 43, 44

**Lesson 1, page 42**
**Lesson 2, page 43**
**Lesson 3, page 44**
**Lesson 4, review and evaluation**

## Lesson 1, page 42

### Objectives
- Identifies letter *r* in printed words.
- Traces and writes manuscript letter *r* and phrases that contain *r*.

### Preparation
*Ahead of time.* Prepare labels for objects or areas in your classroom. The following are suggested because they contain the letter *r*: *chalkboard, drinking fountain, pencil sharpener, door, calendar, library, art center, reading center.* Many other items in your classroom can also be labeled. Mount the labels next to each object or area. Plan to leave them there so children will learn some of these words. Children will enjoy being able to read long words, such as *calendar.*

*Class time.* Point out the labels containing the letter *r* in examples located around the classroom. Read each one for pupils and ask for volunteers to identify the letter *r* in each.

### Teaching

Have pupils turn to page 42 and locate the pictures at the top of the page. Identify each picture and guide pupils in locating and underlining the letter *r* in each label.

Call attention to the writing lines and give the following directions as pupils study the models for the letter *r*:

a raccoon    an orange    a dinosaur

a carrot

red cherries

a fork

a feather

four roosters

page 42

—Start at the middle line; slant down to the bottom line; retrace up; make a hump to the right, and stop. [Down, up, and a roof.]

Give the directions again as pupils begin to trace and write the letter *r* on the writing lines. Repeat the directions as necessary.

Call attention to the pictures on the lower part of the page. Discuss each of the pictures and its label.

Point out that there are two words in each label and that pupils should remember to leave the proper amount of space between words as they write. Then allow pupils time to trace and write the labels independently. Have them note the spacing and formation of the letters, especially of the letter *r*. Provide extra guidance for any children who need it.

D'Nealian Handwriting, Book 1. © Scott, Foresman and Company.

69

# Lesson 2, page 43

## Objectives

- Identifies letter *n* in printed words.
- Traces and writes manuscript letter *n* and phrases that contain *n*.
- Draws a picture of a friend.

## Preparation

*Ahead of time.* Select names containing the letter *n* from your class list. Use names in which the letter *n* occurs in a position other than the initial position. Write the names low on the chalkboard, so that children may reach them.

*Class time.* Identify the names on the chalkboard. Ask the children whose names you read to come to the board. Instruct each child to underline the letter *n* in his or her own name. Review the position of *n* in each name.

## Teaching ▬▬▬▬▬▬▬▬▬

Have pupils turn to page 43 and look at the parts of the letter *n* as you give the following directions:

—Start at the middle line; slant down to the bottom line; retrace up to the middle line; make a hump to the right; slant down to the bottom line, and swing up.

[Down, up, hump, and a monkey tail].

Give the directions again as children begin to trace and write the letter *n* on the writing lines. Point out that this letter begins just like the letter *r*.

Tell pupils to locate the pictures below the writing lines. Identify the labels for pupils, and explain that this whole page deals with friends. Have pupils trace and write the two labels, paying close attention to word spacing and the formation of the letter *n*.

Point out the letters near the middle of the page. Explain that pupils have already learned all these letters. Review the formation of any letters children are unsure of.

Direct attention to the picture and label below the letters. Read the label. Instruct pupils to write the

words *lots of friends* on the writing line. Explain that this phrase has three words, and pupils should be careful to leave the appropriate space. Read the label to the right (*my friend*) and tell pupils to draw a picture of their own friend in the space provided.

---

name

*n n n* n n    *n*

*n*    *n*

two friends

*two friends*

four friends

*four friends*

*d e f i l n o r s t*

lots of friends

my friend

# Lesson 3, page 44

## Objectives
- Identifies letter *m* in printed words.
- Traces and writes manuscript letter *m* and words that contain *m*.
- Uses eye-hand coordination to draw a line between parallel curved lines.

## Preparation
*Ahead of time.* Select names of streets in the school neighborhood that contain the letter *m*. Write the street names on the board.

*Class time.* Read the street names to children. Guide them in locating and underlining the letter *m*.

## Teaching
Have children turn to page 44 and locate the models of the letter *m*. Point out that this letter begins like the letter *n*, but the letter *m* has one more hump. Ask students to look at the models while you give the directions:

—Start at the middle line; slant down to the bottom line; retrace up to the middle line; make a hump to the right; slant down to the bottom line; retrace up; make another hump to the right; slant down to the bottom line, and swing up.

[Down, up, hump, hump, and a monkey tail.]

Repeat the directions as many times as necessary while children trace and write the letter *m* on the first two writing lines.

Call attention to the pictures and labels below the writing lines. Discuss the pictures and identify the labels. Ask pupils if any of these labels have more than one word (no). Then ask how they know that none of the labels have more than one word (none of the labels have a word space). Instruct pupils to trace and write each label, paying particular attention to the formation of the letter *m* and the spacing between letters within a word. Remind pupils not to leave too much space between letters.

Have children put their pencils on the mouse in the

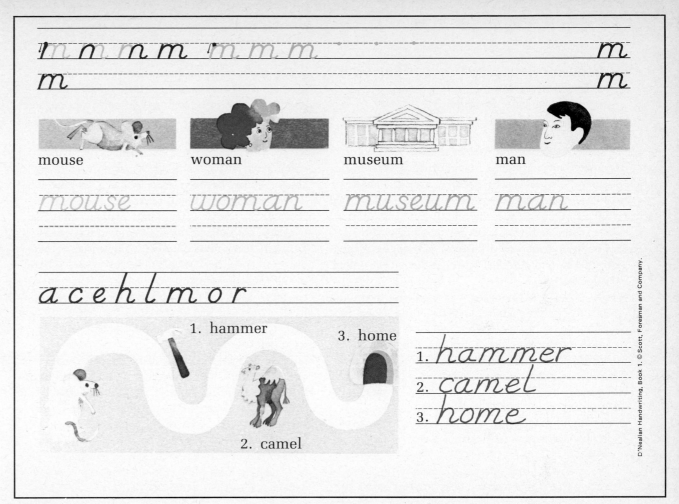

page 44

lower left-hand corner of the page. Direct children to draw a line showing the path the mouse must take to get home, without touching any lines.

Point out the letters on the writing line, telling pupils that they have learned all these letters. Review the formation of any letters that cause problems for children in your class.

Look back with children at the path the mouse took to get home. Ask pupils what the mouse passed first (hammer). Ask what the mouse passed next (camel).

Then ask where the mouse went last (home). Tell children to write the names of the places the mouse went in order on the writing lines to the right. Point out that, if they need help forming a manuscript letter, they can look at the letters on the writing line. Every letter they will need can be found there. If necessary, remind children of the differences between some letters set in type and those they write (a, for example). Review the sequence of places the mouse went when children have finished.

# Lesson 4, review and evaluation

## Objectives
- Writes lower-case manuscript letters introduced up to this point in program.
- Evaluates own letter formation.

## Preparation

*Ahead of time.* Look back at the instructions for forming the twenty-one letters learned thus far in this program. Be prepared to demonstrate these letters on the chalkboard, while simultaneously giving directions similar to those given earlier in this *Teacher's Edition.* Have writing paper available for each pupil.

For another method of introducing and reinforcing letter formation, see the activity section at the end of this lesson.

*Class time.* Distribute the writing paper. Explain to pupils that you are going to review all the letters they have learned so far. Tell them that they still have not learned the whole alphabet, but that they may be surprised at how many letters they have learned in manuscript handwriting.

## Teaching, review and evaluation

Because this will entail a lot of writing for youngsters, you may wish to break it up into several sittings during the day.

Proceed with introducing the letters in the order they are presented in the pupils' book. Present each letter on the chalkboard, accompanying it with oral directions for writing the letter. Give pupils time to write the letter three times. Direct pupils to use their very best handwriting as they write three of each letter on the paper. Explain that pupils will later decide which of the three examples for each letter was best. Children may tend to erase quite a bit in an attempt to be particularly neat. Encourage them not to erase their writing, but rather to try to improve on the next attempt of that letter.

Explain that children should use up all of the space on one line before going on to the next line. If they can only fit two of one letter on one line, they may put the third example of that letter on the next line.

After introducing and having children write a, d, o, g, c, e, and s, pause for a moment. Ask children how all these letters are similar or alike. (They all begin in about the same place, and the beginning motion is in the same direction.)

Continue in this manner, reviewing the rest of the letters with pupils. After introducing and having children write f, b, l, t, h, and k, ask children about the similarities between these letters. (They are all tall letters, and most of them—except for f—begin with a downward stroke.) After children have written i, u, w, and y, ask them about similarities in these letters. (All start at the middle line with a downstroke that curves to the right.) After pupils write j, ask what g, y, and j have in common. (All have tails that curl to the left.) Look for similarities with pupils after they have written r, n, and m. (All begin at the middle line with a downstroke, then an upstroke that starts to curve right.)

When you have reviewed all of the letters, ask children to look back at the top of their paper. Tell them to look at the three a's they wrote, decide which is best, and circle it. Tell pupils to continue in this manner with each letter reviewed, selecting the best letter from each group of three.

When pupils have finished, collect their papers. At a later time, you may find it interesting to review their papers, noting their evaluations of their own handwriting.

## Activities

*Letter introduction and review.* If available, you will find that the overhead projector is a wonderful tool to use in the teaching of handwriting. It not only gives an easily visible image of the letters, but it also allows the teacher to have eye contact with pupils. Children also love to practice their handwriting on the overhead projector.

*Alphabet pretzels.* Children will really feel that they have mastered the formation of manuscript letters when they actually get to eat those same letters that once may have given them some problems. This alphabet pretzel recipe makes 18 to 24 pretzel letters.

½ c. water  
1 pkg. dry yeast      dissolve  
4 c. flour  
1 tbsp. sugar      mix  
1 tsp. salt  
1 egg beaten slightly with 1 tbsp. water  
Coarse-grain salt (kosher salt is dandy)

With a large spoon, work flour mixture into yeast mixture in a large bowl. When about 3 cups of flour mix have been worked in, begin to knead the mixture on a counter top while working in the remaining flour mix. Divide the dough into 18–24 parts. Shape the dough into letters and place on greased pans. Paint the letters with egg-water mixture and sprinkle salt on them. Bake 25 minutes, or until golden brown, at 425°F.

*Bumpy letters.* On cardboard write a large model of a manuscript letter. Then dot white liquid glue every half-inch or so on the letter form. Provide directional arrows and a beginning dot. When the letters are dry, children may trace them with their fingers for extra reinforcement of letters they are unsure of.

# SECTION 12

**pages 45, 46, 47**

Lesson 1, page 45
Lesson 2, preparation for page 46
Lesson 3, page 46
Lesson 4, page 47

## Lesson 1, page 45

### Objectives

- Identifies letter *p* in printed words.
- Traces and writes manuscript letter *p* and words that contain *p*.
- Draws a picture.

### Preparation

*Ahead of time.* Select any commercial game boxes that have the letter *p* on the cover. These game boxes may be chosen from your supply of rainy-day games.

*Class time.* Display the game boxes, and guide pupils in locating the letter *p* within the words on the box covers.

### Teaching

Have pupils turn to page 45 and locate the pictures at the top of the page. Discuss the pictures and labels. Instruct pupils to locate and underline the letter *p* within the labels.

Direct attention to the model letters on the writing lines. Ask pupils to look at the parts of the letter as you give the directions:

—Start at the middle line; slant down half a line below the bottom line; retrace up; go right around, down to the bottom line, and close.
[Down under water, up, around, and a tummy.]

Give the directions again as pupils begin to trace and write the letter *p* on the writing line following the models. Remind pupils that part of the letter *p* hangs

page 45

below the bottom line. Repeat the directions for those who need extra guidance while practicing.

Call attention to the pictures and labels below the writing line. Discuss these pictures, mentioning that some people have guppies or puppies for pets. Ask if anyone in the class has either or both of these kinds of pets at home. Instruct pupils to trace the word *guppies* and then write it independently. Remind them to watch the formation of the letter *p*. Tell them to follow the same procedure with the label *puppies*.

When pupils have finished, tell them that they now have a chance to show what pet or pets they like. Direct pupils to use the space on the right to draw pictures of pets they like.

## Lesson 2, preparation for page 46

**Objectives**
- Recognizes and collects pictures of a given color.
- Uses eye-hand coordination to cut and paste pictures

**Teaching, preparation for page 46**

*Ahead of time.* Have on hand a selection of old magazines or catalogs. You will need at least eight magazines. Label eight sheets of large white construction paper, each with a different one of the following color names: *red, orange, blue, yellow, brown, purple, black, green.* If possible, get sample cards of various shades of these colors from a paint or hardware store. Paste these cards near the top of the appropriately labeled construction paper sheet. Also provide scissors and paste.

*Class time.* Display the construction paper sheets with the color labels on them. Explain to pupils that very often they will see various shades of the same color. If you have color samples from a paint store, point out the various shades at the top of one of the sheets.

Divide the class into eight groups. Assign each group one of the eight colors, and give them a construction paper sheet. Explain that they will be looking in magazines for pictures of anything that is their assigned color. Tell them that when they cut out a picture in their color, they should paste it on their sheet of construction paper.

Distribute the magazines or catalogs, scissors, and paste.

Later, provide time for each group to share its color sheet and the pictures pasted on it.

If you wish, you may save the color sheets for an activity at the end of the next lesson.

## Lesson 3, page 46

**Objectives**
- Uses visual discrimination to match colors and names of colors.

page 46

- Writes appropriate label below a picture.

**Teaching** ━━━━━━━━━

Have pupils turn to page 46. With pupils, identify the color words at the top of the page. Instruct children to write the correct color word beneath each stack of T-shirts. Some children may need guidance at first, but most will be able to complete the page on their own.

**Activities**

*Color identification.* Display a sheet of colored construction paper or the color-sample sheets made by the class in Lesson 2 of this section. Then ask volunteers to name objects in the classroom that are the same color. Continue color identification of objects until the colors red, orange, blue, yellow, brown, purple, black, and green are emphasized. Let pupils write color labels for the objects they identify.

*I spy.* Begin this color identification game by saying "I see something yellow" (or any of the eight colors emphasized). Children may then ask questions that would receive a yes or no answer, such as, "Is it large?" When they think they have enough clues, they may try to name the object. The person who guesses the object is the leader of the next game.

## Lesson 4, page 47

### Objectives
- Identifies letter *q* in printed words.
- Traces and writes the letter *q* and phrases containing *q*.

### Teaching

Have children turn to page 47 and identify the pictures at the top of the page. Discuss the pictures and their labels with children. Guide children in locating and underlining the letter *q* in the word *queen*, and ask them to underline *q* in the next two labels. Point out that *q* is a letter that is not used often and is almost always followed by the letter *u*.

Direct attention to the models of the letter *q* on the writing lines. Tell pupils to look at the parts of the letter *q* while you give the following directions:
—Start at the middle line; go left around, down to the bottom line, around and up to the beginning; close; retrace down, and go half a line below the bottom line; hook to the right.
[Around, down, up, down, and a backward fishhook under water.]

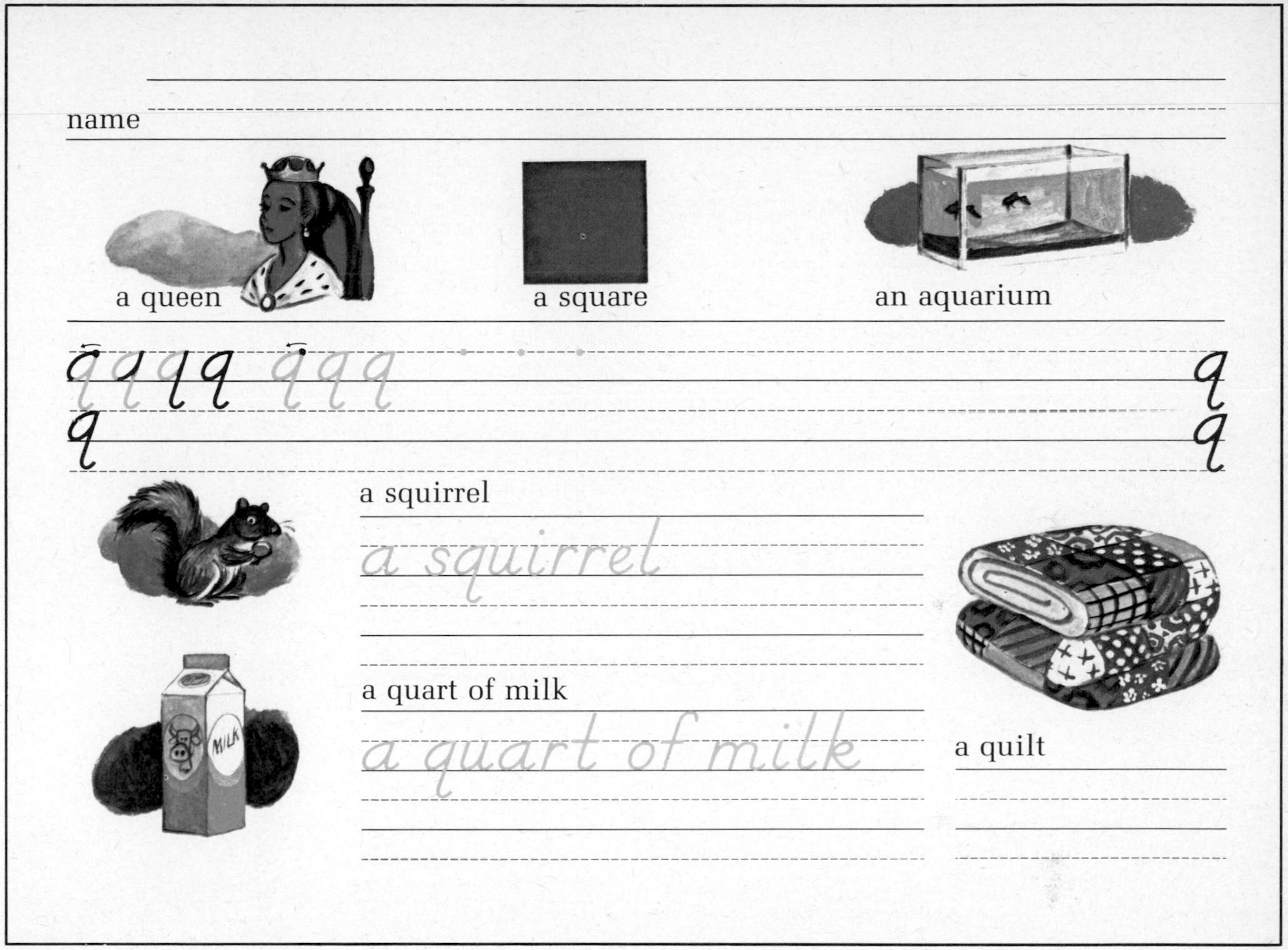

name

a queen

a square

an aquarium

*q q q   q q q*     *q*

*q*     *q*

a squirrel

*a squirrel*

a quart of milk

*a quart of milk*

a quilt

page 47

Point out that *q* is very similar to the letter *g*. Ask if anyone knows how they are different (the tails on the two letters point in opposite directions). You may want to give pupils practice in writing *q* in the air, with their fingers on desk tops, or in sand trays to establish the difference between the letters *q* and *g*.

As pupils trace and write the letter *q*, repeat the directions when necessary.

Call attention to the two pictures on the left. Identify the pictures with pupils and read the labels. Point out

that the second label has four words in it. Have children trace and write the labels, paying close attention to the formation of the letters—especially *q*—and the spacing between words.

Direct attention to the picture on the right. Read the label and instruct children to write *a quilt* on the writing line below the label. Point out that they can find all the letters they will need in other words on the page.

# SECTION 13

**pages 48, 49, 50, 51**

Lesson 1, page 48
Lesson 2, page 49
Lesson 3, page 50
Lesson 4, page 51

## Lesson 1, page 48

### Objectives
- Identifies letter *v* in printed words.
- Traces and writes manuscript letter *v* and words and phrases that contain *v*.

### Teaching

Have pupils turn to page 48. Call attention to the models of the letter *v*, and have children study them as you give the following directions:

—Start at the middle line; slant right down to the bottom line; slant right up to the middle line. [Slant right down, slant right up.]

As pupils begin to trace and write the letter *v* repeat the directions. Allow pupils time to practice writing the letter *v* on the writing lines provided.

Discuss the pictures and identify the labels on the rest of the page. Ask pupils which labels have more than one word *(seven doves, five beavers, and a van)*.

Instruct pupils to trace each label and then write it on their own. Emphasize spacing and letter formation.

### Activities

*Paper bag costumes.* Have pupils cut three holes in the bag for the neck, and arms, or do so yourself. Pupils can then decorate the costumes by coloring or gluing on buttons, pockets, a collar, belt, and so on, using paper, yarn, and cloth scraps. Tell pupils to write a particular letter on their costumes and when you call that letter they are to model their creation for the class.

v v v   v v v · · ·   v

v   V

seven doves

*seven doves*

vases

*vases*

five beavers

*five beavers*

a van

*a van*

vegetables

*vegetables*

violets

*violets*

page 48

*Eye-hand coordination.* Write the first six letters of the alphabet, scattered on the chalkboard at children's eye level. Put a dot next to each letter. Be sure a copy of the alphabet is visible to children. Instruct children to draw straight lines between the dots next to the letters in order. See example.

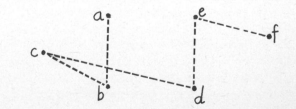

D'Nealian Handwriting, Book 1. © Scott, Foresman and Company.

## Lesson 2, page 49

### Objectives
- Identifies letter *z* in printed words.
- Traces and writes manuscript letter *z* and words and phrases that contain *z*.

### Teaching

Have pupils turn to page 49 and identify the pictures at the top of the page. Read the picture labels and guide pupils in locating the letter *z*. If necessary, write *z* on the chalkboard. Then ask if someone sees that letter in the labels. Have pupils underline the *z*'s in the labels.

Ask pupils to study the models of the letter *z* on the writing line as you give the following directions:
—Start at the middle line; make a bar to the right on the middle line; slant left down to the bottom line; make a bar to the right on the bottom line. [Over, slant down, over.]

Call attention to the pictures on the rest of the page, and read the labels for pupils. Instruct pupils to trace and write the labels, paying close attention to the spacing and the new letter *z*.

### Activities

*Letter identification and review.* On a bulletin board or flannel board, make a tree out of paper or felt. Cut out individual leaves. On the back of each leaf, print a manuscript letter. Children will take turns choosing a leaf. If they can identify the letter on the back, they get to keep the leaf. At the end of the time period, the child with the most leaves wins the game. Depending upon the size of the group, you may wish to provide more than one leaf for each letter.

*Letter recognition.* Make a worksheet similar to the following:

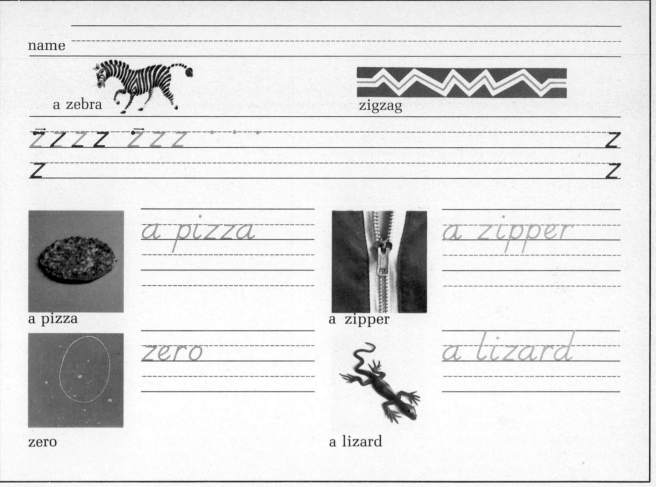

a zebra   zigzag

a pizza   a zipper

zero   a lizard

page 49

At the beginning of each row, provide the letter to be identified and matched. In the rest of the row, provide letters of similar construction (including one to match the letter at the beginning of the row). Instruct children to look at the first letter, find the same letter in that row and underline it. Then have pupils write the cue letter at the end of the row.

# Lesson 3, page 50

## Objectives

- Traces and writes manuscript letter *x* and words and phrases that contain *x*.
- Traces words *first*, *next*, and *last*.
- Writes word *first*, *next*, or *last* below each picture in a set of three to show sequence.

## Teaching ▬

Have pupils turn to page 50. Tell pupils to study the models of the letter *x* as you give the following directions:

—Start at the middle line; slant right down to the bottom line, and swing up. Cross the letter with a slant left.

[Slant down and a monkey tail. Cross with a slant.]

Repeat the directions as often as necessary while pupils trace the row of *x*'s. Allow time for pupils to write the letter *x* independently. Provide assistance, if necessary.

Call attention to the pictures below the writing lines. Read the labels for pupils, pointing out that each has two words. Emphasize formation of letters and spacing as pupils trace and write the labels.

Point out the three words on the writing line near the middle of the page. Read the words *first*, *next*, and *last*. Ask which word has the new letter *x* in it.

Then write the numbers 1, 2, and 3 in order on the chalkboard. Ask a volunteer to tell you which number comes first when counting (1). Write the word *first* beside 1. Ask which number comes next when counting (2). Write *next* beside 2. Then ask which number comes last (3). Write *last* beside 3. Erase the chalkboard.

Call attention to the three pictures of a chick hatching near the bottom of the page. Tell pupils that they must decide which picture shows what took place first, and write the word *first* beneath it. Explain that they should label the picture that shows what happened next with the word *next*, and the picture that shows what took place last with the word *last*.

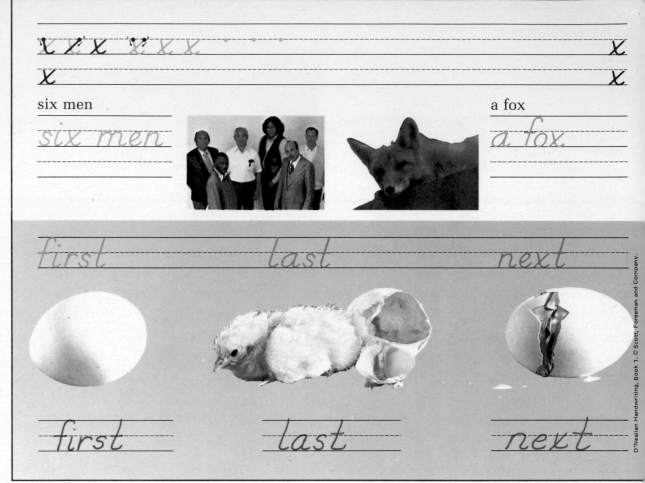

page 50

## Special Populations

Pupils with learning problems require much practice to establish the concepts of *first*, *next*, and *last*. Use physical teaching (handling picture cards, arranging cutout letters, lining up in sequence, stacking books in order, finding pages, and so on). As pupils practice, draw attention to details that give clues as to how parts fit together in sequence. Most class activities can give a review of the concept of sequence.

## Lesson 4, page 51

### Objective
• Writes lower-case manuscript letters and phrases.

### Preparation
*Ahead of time.* Be prepared to review the formation of any of the lower-case manuscript letters.

*Class time.* Explain to pupils that they have learned all of the lower-case manuscript letters of the alphabet.

### Teaching
Have pupils turn to page 51 and identify the letters at the top of the page as the complete alphabet. Tell pupils to write each lower-case letter on the line beneath its model. Circulate around the room, providing assistance with formation of letters where needed.

Call attention to and discuss the pictures and their labels on the second half of the page. Explain that pupils will use most of the letters of the alphabet as they trace and write the phrases independently. Emphasize neatness, correct letter formation, and spacing before children begin. Point out that pupils may use the letters at the top of the page as models.

### Special Populations
Pupils with learning problems may have trouble with this lesson. You may see frustration, confusion with alphabet sequence, turning letters the wrong way, and backward strokes in writing certain letters. Watch for frustration signals, excessive erasing, getting lost on the page, and turning letters backward. Make extra worksheets similar to page 51. Also let pupils work at the chalkboard copying the alphabet you have printed. Listen for misnamed letters (*b* for *d*, for example). Talk about sequence and the way each letter should face.

### Activities
*Alphabet elimination.* This enrichment activity may be used with students who finish the page early. Ask students to find which letters of the

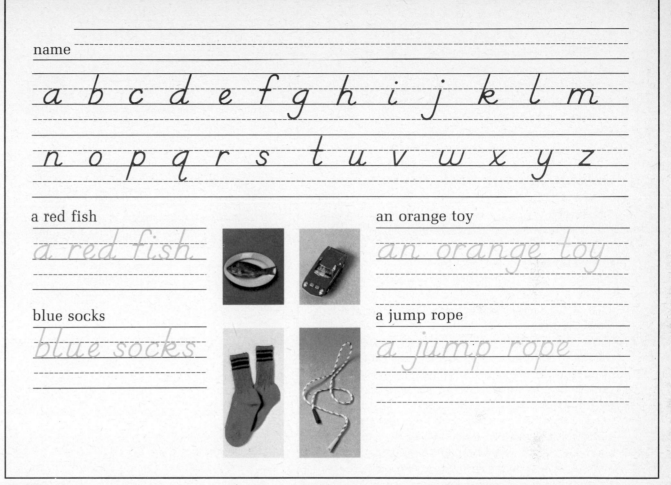

page 51

alphabet they did not write in the four phrases on the bottom half of the page (*q, v, w, x, z*).

*Funny pictures.* Distribute 9- by-12-inch newsprint to children. Tell them to choose one letter they have learned and write it in very large print on the paper. Point out that the letter they have written might look very much like a familiar object or animal. Encourage discussion of objects some letters look like. Then ask children to add details to the letters to make them look like an object or an animal. Demonstrate on the chalkboard by starting with a letter and adding a few details to form a picture. See examples.

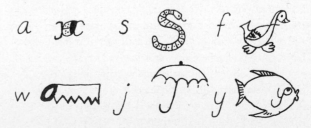

# SECTION 14

pages 52, 53, 54

**Lesson 1, page 52**
**Lesson 2, review**
**Lesson 3, page 53**
**Lesson 4, page 54**

## Lesson 1, page 52

### Objective

• Writes words that are names for numbers.

### Preparation

*Ahead of time.*  Be prepared to review the formation of any letters children have learned. Have on hand some counters used in your math program (Popsicle sticks, buttons, and so on).

*Class time.*  Write the number 0 on the chalkboard, and ask students how many counters you should hold up to show this number (0).  Introduce the number word *zero*, explaining that this is the word that stands for the number 0.  Display one counter and ask a volunteer to come to the chalkboard and write the number that shows how many you are holding.  Then ask if anyone can write the number word *one*.  If no one can, write it on the chalkboard yourself.  Continue in this manner, reviewing the numbers 2–10 and introducing the corresponding number words.

page 52

### Teaching ▬▬▬▬▬▬▬▬

Have pupils turn to page 52.  Ask them to locate the row of numbers at the top of the page.

Explain that pupils will write all the number words from *zero* through *ten* on this page.  Direct attention to the first row of pictures and writing lines.  Ask pupils how many objects they see in the first picture (0).  Point out that zero objects are shown in the first picture, and the number word next to the picture is *zero*.  Ask children to trace *zero* and write it on the blank writing line.

Continue guiding pupils through the first row by discussing the number of objects in each picture and instructing them to trace and write the number word.

Pupils should be able to complete the page independently.  Caution them to count the objects in each picture carefully.  Emphasize correct letter formation.  Point out that the last picture does not have a number word beside it.  Pupils are to count the objects and write the correct word.

## Lesson 2, review

### Objective

• Writes words that are names for a number.

### Preparation

*Ahead of time.*  Make a worksheet like the one below.  Have a worksheet and crayons for each child.

80

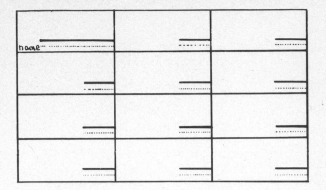

## Teaching, review

Distribute the worksheets and crayons to children. Have pupils turn to page 52 in their books so that they can see how to spell each number word.

Ask children to write their names in the first section of the worksheet. Instruct pupils to draw a set of objects in each section. They should draw the sets in numerical order from zero to ten. Then have children write the number word in each section to show how many objects there are. For example, the first section after the name box will have *zero* in it. The last section should have *ten* written in it and should picture ten small objects.

Children do not have to draw the same objects in each section.

## Lesson 3, page 53

### Objective
• Writes appropriate label for each part of a picture.

### Preparation
*Ahead of time.* Be prepared to review any of the letters at the top of page 53.

### Teaching
Have pupils turn to page 53. Explain that the letters at the top of the page will be used to write words on the page. Review any letters that cause difficulty for pupils.

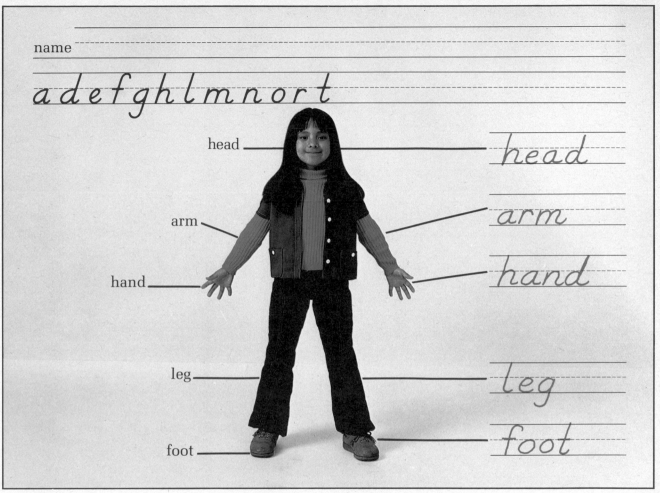

page 53

Direct attention to the picture, and ask pupils to identify each label. Make sure that children notice the pointer leading from each label to the corresponding body part.

After sufficient discussion of the labels, tell pupils to label the parts of the body. Ask what the first arrow at the left points to and what label belongs on the first writing line *(head)*. Have pupils write *head*, referring to the model letters at the top of the page if necessary. Allow pupils to continue independently.

### Special Populations
Pupils with learning problems must memorize body cues to recall which hand is right or left. Some children must wear a ring, wristwatch, or bracelet to recall which is which. It is easy to use the child's writing hand as the point of reference. For right-handed pupils, the homonyms help in naming—the *right* hand is the *writing* hand. Left-handed children learn that the right hand is the *other hand*. Some children tell left from right by clues in the classroom (wall clock, pencil sharpener, teacher's desk.

Once pupils know their left hand from their right hand on themselves, transferring this knowledge to someone facing the opposite way is difficult. Persons in pictures present a mirror image in which left and right are reversed. Keep in mind that if you ask pupils to find the right side of the picture on page 53, they are finding the *left side* of the child's body.

Most primary pupils need physical learning to master left/right body concepts. Have pupils choose partners and stand facing each other. Tie colored yarn on each child's left wrist. Teach them to raise the left hand or right hand on command. Talk about each child feeling his or her hand rise while watching the partner's opposite hand do the same. Each hand is left or right, but the partner's hands are turned around (mirror image).

Then have partners stand side by side facing the same direction and show how all left and right hands are now on the same body sides. Practice the concept of left and right until pupils understand where body sides are located in a picture or mirror.

## Lesson 4, page 54

### Objectives
- Classifies pictured animals by size.
- Writes name of an animal below appropriate heading (*big* or *little*).
- Writes a sample of handwriting on page 111.

### Teaching
Have pupils turn to page 54. Discuss the pictures at the top of the page and identify their labels.

Ask pupils which of these animals they consider to be very big and which they think of as little. Point out and identify the labels above the writing lines on the bottom half of the page. Instruct pupils to write the names of the animals that are big below the word *big* and the names of the animals that are little below the word *little*.

When pupils have finished writing, instruct them to turn to page 111. Point out that they have already

page 54

written on some lines of this page earlier in the year.

Ask pupils to locate the first blank writing line that has a round dot at the beginning. Explain that they are going to write in their best handwriting the numbers 0 through 10. Emphasize correct number formation.

When pupils have finished writing the row of numbers, tell them to find the next round dot at the beginning of a blank writing line. Explain that they will use their best handwriting to write their name on this line. When pupils have finished writing their

names, ask if they think they have improved in writing numbers and their names since the first of the year.

Direct attention to the last blank writing line that begins with a round dot. Discuss the pictures above this writing line and identify the labels. Point out the number of words in each phrase. Explain that they are to write *a big sandwich* and *a pile of junk* on the writing lines beginning with the round dot. Emphasize correct letter formation, spacing, and neatness.

D'Nealian Handwriting, Book 1. © Scott, Foresman and Company.

# SECTION 15

**Pages 55, 56, 57**

**Lesson 1, page 55**
**Lesson 2, page 56**
**Lesson 3, page 57**
**Lesson 4, review and evaluation**

## Lesson 1, page 55

### Objectives
- Identifies *C* and *c* in printed words.
- Traces and writes manuscript letter *C* and names that begin with the letter *C*.
- Develops concept that a name begins with a capital letter.

### Preparation
*Ahead of time.* Write *c* and *C* on the board.
*Class time.* Review the formation of *c*, emphasizing that it starts near the middle line and uses only one-half of the writing line. Point out that the capital letter *C* is larger and begins near the top line.

### Teaching

Have pupils turn to page 55. Call attention to the models of *c* and *C* in the box at the top of the page. Note the likenesses between them.

Ask pupils to look at the parts of the letter *C* as you give the following directions:
—Start a little below the top line; go up to the top line, go left around, down to the bottom line; curve right and stop.
[Curved high start, around, down, up, and stop.]

Repeat the directions as pupils trace and write the letter *C* on the writing lines. Emphasize the beginning point of the letter.

Explain that names always begin with a capital

page 55

letter. Remind pupils that their own names begin with a capital letter, although it may not be *C*. Identify and write on the board pupils' names that do begin with *C*.

Discuss the names of the people pictured on the page. Guide pupils in locating and underlining *C* and *c* in the printed names near each picture. This will be the last time these instructions will be included. In subsequent lessons, you may wish to continue this type of activity on your own.

Point out that each name begins with a *C* and that only the first letter of each name is a capital. Indicate that some names have the lower-case letter *c* in them, but that they all *begin* with a capital *C*.

Instruct pupils to trace each name and to write it on the blank writing line. Most students will be able to complete the page independently. Provide assistance where necessary.

83

# Lesson 2, page 56

## Objectives
- Traces and writes manuscript letter *G* and names that begin with the letter *G*.
- Develops concept that a name in a phrase begins with a capital letter.

## Preparation
*Ahead of time.* Write *g* and *G* on the board.

*Class time.* Review the formation of the lower-case letter *g*. Tell students that they will learn to write the capital letter *G* in this lesson. Point out the differences between the lower-case and capital forms of the letter. Remind students that capital letters are always used when writing the first letter of a name. Ask if anyone in the class has a name that begins with *G*. If so, write it on the board and underline the capital *G*.

## Teaching
Have pupils turn to page 56 and locate the letters *g* and *G* in the box at the top of the page. Point out that *G* is similar to *C*. Ask pupils to look at the parts of the letter *G* as you give the following directions:

—Start a little below the top line; go up to the top line; go left around, down to the bottom line; curve right, up to the middle line; make a bar to the left. [Curved high start, around, down, up, and over left.]

Repeat the directions as necessary while pupils trace and write *G* on the first two writing lines.

Discuss the pictures of girl and the dog in the first row. Identify each name and note that it begins with a capital letter. Point out that the last picture in the row shows Gigi and George together. Indicate that even though Gigi is not the first name in the label, it still begins with a capital *G*. Emphasize that names always begin with a capital letter no matter where they appear. Ask students if they see the

page 56

lower-case *g* in any of the names. Guide students in pointing out that the lower-case form seldom appears at the beginning of a name.

Identify the names of the boy and the cat pictured in the second row. Point out that every name begins with a capital letter. Instruct pupils to trace and write the names. Emphasize correct formation of

letters—especially *G*. Remind students that two labels have more than one word and that pupils should remember to provide the proper spacing.

Most students will be able to complete the page independently. Provide assistance where necessary.

## Lesson 3, page 57

**Objective**

• Develops concept that a sentence may begin with
a a capital letter and end with a period.

**Preparation**

*Class time*. Review formation of the letters *C* and
*G*, pointing out the similar construction of the letters.
Ask students to tell what they have learned about
where they should use a capital letter (the beginning
letter of a name).

Tell students that they will now learn about
another situation in which they should always use
a capital.

**Teaching** ■■■■■■■

Have pupils turn to page 57. Discuss the picture
and read the sentence at the top of the page for
pupils. Explain that the words you just read express
a complete idea. Guide pupils in understanding that
a sentence is a group of words that give a complete
thought. Do not expect every student to understand
the concept of complete sentences at this time.

Point out that *Giraffes* is the first word in the
sentence and that it begins with a capital letter.
Explain that every sentence begins with a capital
letter—whether it begins with a name or not. Ask
students to look at the end of the sentence and tell
them that the dot at the end is called a *period*. Point
out that sentences usually end with a period.

Tell pupils to trace and write each sentence on the
page. Have them pay close attention to the letter
formation and spacing between words. Remind
pupils to include the period at the end of each
sentence.

Most pupils will be able to complete the page
independently. However, if someone needs help, be
prepared to provide assistance.

name

Giraffes are big animals.

*Giraffes are big animals.*

Camels are big too.

*Camels are big too.*

Caterpillars are little.

*Caterpillars are little.*

page 57

**Activities**

*Capital letter usage*. To reinforce the concepts that
the first letter of a name is always capitalized and the
first letter of the initial word in a sentence is always
capitalized, provide oral activities such as the following. Read sentences to pupils, asking them to repeat
the words that should begin with a capital letter.
Make sure the sentences do not use unfamiliar rules
of capitalization. Here are some sample sentences.

—Mary went to the store.
—She bought a can of soup.
—She also bought a present for Tom.
—Gigi and George played with Carol.
—They asked Greg and Cecelia to play.

*Sentence identification*. Read sentences and
phrases to pupils. Have volunteers tell you which
are sentences and which are only phrases.

# Lesson 4, review and evaluation

## Objectives
- Writes names beginning with a capital letter.
- Writes sentences beginning with a capital letter and ending with a period.

## Preparation
*Ahead of time*. Have available handwriting paper for each child. Choose names of children in your class beginning with the letters *C* and *G*. If there are none, choose names the children have written on pages 55 and 56. Be prepared to write an experience story with children using these names. You may plan to present the story on the chalkboard, on the overhead projector, or on chart paper.

Write the names on the chalkboard. The activity can be particularly exciting if children whose names begin with *C* or *G* contribute sentences about themselves and their experiences.

Plan to center the story around a theme with which children are familiar. Perhaps you took a field trip recently and would like to review that experience. If a holiday is in the near future or has just passed, you might relate the story to that. Other suggested topics for the story might be a class play or just everyday school experiences. Limit the story to only a few sentences. Be sure the sentences will begin with the letter *C* or *G*.

## Teaching, review and evaluation
Distribute handwriting paper to students and explain that the class will write a short story about characters with the names you have chosen.

Once the theme is decided upon, encourage children to contribute the sentences. As you write each sentence, explain any changes you make from the original sentence a pupil may have contributed. Be careful not to alter pupils' sentences too much.

Ask children to write each sentence as you do. Remind them that each sentence begins with a capital letter and ends with a period. Emphasize correct letter formation. Tell them to also use a capital letter when writing names. Circulate among children, when possible, to assist with locating the correct line, letter formation, and proper spacing.

A finished story might look like this:

Carlos and Cathy went to the museum.
Cathy liked the rocks.
Carlos liked the old hats.

When the class story is complete and everyone has finished writing, ask children to get out their red, blue, and green crayons. Explain that you are going to read each sentence in the story. Whenever they see a period in their story, they are to circle it in red. Next, ask a volunteer to reread the story, and tell pupils to underline with green each capital letter that begins a sentence. Ask another volunteer to reread the story one more time. This time instruct pupils to underline with blue the capital letters that begin names.

When everyone has finished, discuss the reason each capital letter was used. If a name was used at the beginning of a sentence, explain that it should have both a green and a blue line under it.

If you wish, you may allow pupils time to draw a picture to accompany the story.

## Activities
*Experience stories*. Provide lots of opportunities for children to write experience stories as a group. You might pass out a series of pictures to groups of children. Have each group combine their talents to produce a sentence that describes the picture. Provide help with spelling. When everyone is finished, display the pictures in order. Ask a volunteer from each group to read their sentence.

*Sentence scramble*. Copy sentences from a story children have read in their reading program. Write each sentence on a different color of construction paper. Cut the sentences into phrases. Then have individuals or small groups put the sentences back in order. When reviewing their work, point out that each sentence begins with a capital letter.

*Sentence structure*. Give each pupil in a group a word or phrase that is part of a sentence. Have pupils hold their section of the sentence and stand in the correct order. After their sentence has been revealed to the rest of the class, ask one or two of the students to sit down. Then ask if the remaining words still make a complete sentence. If class members decide that they do not, ask the people holding the missing parts to rejoin the others to complete their sentence.

# SECTION 16

pages 58, 59, 60, 61

## Lesson 1, page 58

### Objective
• Traces and writes manuscript letter *O* and words and sentences that contain *O*.

### Preparation
*Ahead of time.* Write *o* and *O* on the board.

*Class time.* Review the formation of *o*, emphasizing that it begins near the middle line and uses only one-half the writing line. Note the likenesses between *o* and *O*. Point out that *O* takes up the whole line.

### Teaching ▬▬▬▬

Have children turn to page 58 and find the box at the top of the page containing *o* and *O*.

Ask pupils to look at the parts of the letter *O* next to the box as you give the following directions:
—Start at the top line; go left around, down to the bottom line, around and up to the beginning; close. [Curved high start, around, down, up, and close.]

Repeat the directions as necessary while pupils trace and write the letter *O*. Emphasize the starting point at the top line. Some pupils may notice the similarity between the letter *O* and the number 0 (zero). Remind them that the letter is called "O," and the number is called "zero."

Call attention to the pictures and identify the people pictured as Oscar and Ophelia. Point out that these names both begin with capital *O*. Allow time for pupils to trace and write the names.

page 58

Discuss the picture to the left and read the sentences. Ask pupils to give two reasons for the use of the capital letter in these sentences (a capital at beginning of a name and at the beginning of a sentence). Instruct pupils to trace and write each sentence. Have them pay particular attention to the capital *O* and the spacing between words. Remind pupils that each sentence has a period at the end. Circulate among students to provide assistance if necessary.

### Activity
*Collage.* Give children magazines, scissors, paste, and paper. Have them write *O* at the top of the paper. Instruct them to cut out pictures of objects that are the shape of the letter *O* and paste them on the sheet of paper. Tell pupils that the pictures may overlap slightly.

## Lesson 2, page 59

### Objective
- Traces and writes manuscript letter *Q* and a word and a sentence that begin with *Q*.

### Preparation
*Ahead of time.* Write *q* and *Q* on the board.

*Class time.* Review the formation of *q* and point out the capital form of the letter. Note the differences between the two letters.

### Teaching
Have pupils turn to page 59 and locate the box containing *q* and *Q*. Ask pupils to look at the parts of *Q* next to the box as you give the following directions:

—Start at the top line; go left around, down to the bottom line, around and up to the beginning; close. Start below the middle line; slant right across the bottom of the letter, and swing up.
[Curved high start, around, down, up, close. Add a monkey tail.]

Point out that the first part of the letter is just like *O*. Repeat the directions as necessary while pupils trace and write *Q* on the writing lines.

Read the word *Quack* for students and have them trace it. Explain that the printed label shows the other duck is also saying "Quack." Instruct pupils to write the word independently, using the letters they traced as a model.

Call attention to the sleeping duck and identify the cover on the bed as a quilt. Read the sentence for pupils. Allow them to trace and write the sentence independently. Remind them that the sentence begins with a capital and ends with a period.

page 59

### Special Populations
Pupils with learning problems will have trouble handling the directionality and similar shapes of *p*, *q*, *g*, and *y*. Provide extra chalkboard practice for the pupils who reverse and have trouble remembering directionality. Watch for backward strokes on *Q*. Hold the child's writing hand as you guide the pencil in the right direction. Have the pupil say the letter name while tracing, then do the same while copying.

### Activity
*Funny pictures.* Provide paper and crayons for children. Have them write a large capital letter *C*, *G*, *O*, or *Q* on the paper. Then tell them to add details to the letter to make a funny picture. If necessary, point out that all the letters are curved, and any one of them could look like almost anything that is round. Encourage originality and creativity. Display all completed masterpieces.

### Objective
• Traces and writes manuscript letter *S* and sentences that contain *S*.

### Preparation
*Ahead of time.* Write *s* and *S* on the board.

*Class time.* Review the formation of *s,* emphasizing its beginning point and size. Point out how similar the capital *S* is to the lower-case, but also note that it is taller and begins near the top line.

### Teaching
Have students turn to page 60 and locate *s* and *S* in the box. Ask students to look at the parts of *S* as you give these directions.

—Start a little below the top line; go up to the top line; go left around, down to the middle line; then go right around, down to the bottom line; curve left, up, and stop.

[Curved high start, around left, and a snake tail.]

Repeat the directions as necessary while pupils trace and write *S*.

Direct attention to the picture and read the sentences for pupils. After you have read the second sentence, ask pupils to tell you who the word *She* refers to (Sue). Point out that *She* is not her name, but it is the first word in the sentence and, therefore, must begin with a capital letter.

Instruct pupils to trace and write the sentences independently. Have them pay attention to the formation of capital *S*, the spacing between words, and the period at the end of each sentence. Provide assistance where needed.

### Special Populations
Pupils with learning problems may have difficulty writing letters and numbers that begin with the curved right-to-left top stroke (*S,* G, and C, for example). The letter *S* involves three changes of direction in hand movement. Making the pencil

Sue owns a bookstore.

She sells books.

page 60

turn the corner at the right time is very difficult for some children. Hold the child's hand firmly as you guide the pencil around the curves of *S*. Provide a good deal of chalkboard practice, starting with large letters to let the pupils use large motions at first. Gradually reduce the size of *S* on the board until pupils are comfortable with smaller work. Then transfer this practice to paper. Have pupils say the letter name as they trace and copy. Watch for

frustration signals and trouble transferring from the chalkboard to paper.

### Activity
*Eye-hand coordination.* Provide children with opportunities to trace around models of shapes or letters. The models may be made from cardboard. Children may trace with chalk at the chalkboard or with felt-tip pens or pencils at their desks.

# Lesson 4, page 61

## Objectives
- Writes letters *C, G, O, Q, S.*
- Writes names in the order in which they appear along a pathway.

## Preparation
*Ahead of time.* Be prepared to review the formation of any letter to be written on page 61—especially the capital letters.

## Teaching
Have pupils turn to page 61. Indicate that the five capital letters at the top of the page are those they have learned recently. Review any that pose a problem for members of your class. Direct attention to the row of lower-case letters. Explain that these are letters they will use while writing on this page. Ask pupils to study all the letters for a minute and tell you which capital letters do not have their lower-case manuscript partners on the page *(C, Q).*

Call attention to the path that begins in the lower left-hand corner. Explain that the two people are going shopping. Identify the places the shoppers will go, in order, and explain that the sign at each place has capital letters at the beginning of words. Instruct pupils to write on the numbered writing lines the name of each place in the order the shoppers will go to them. Remind pupils that they may find all the letters they will need at the top of the page. Caution them that one word does not begin with a capital.

Allow students to proceed independently, but provide assistance when necessary.

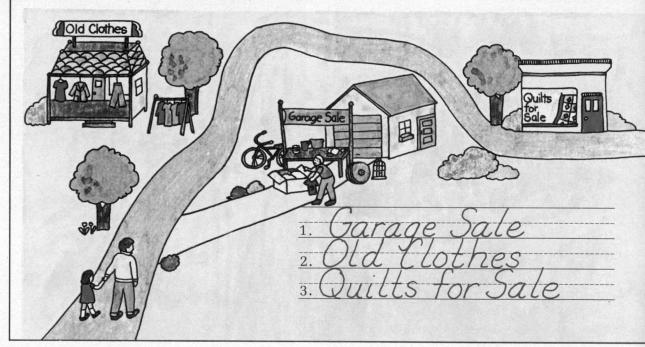

page 61

## Activities
*Visual memory and sequential order.* Write a series of letters on the chalkboard or put them on a flannel board. Ask children to close their eyes while you rearrange the order of the letters. Then ask children which letter is out of order. Begin by using three or four letters and changing the position of only one. As children improve, you may increase the number of letters and changes or take out letters.

*Mirror image.* Provide a simple path for children to trace on a piece of cardboard, laminated or covered with acetate. Children will use crayons to trace the path. The difficult part is that they should look in a mirror as they draw a line along the path. When children have finished, ask if they discovered anything. The reflection in the mirror will show their movements backwards.

# SECTION 17

**Pages 62, 63, 64**

Lesson 1, page 62
Lesson 2, page 63
Lesson 3, preparation for page 64
Lesson 4, page 64

## Lesson 1, page 62

### Objectives
• Traces and writes manuscript letter *I* and sentences that begin with *I*.
• Completes a sentence by choosing a word.

### Preparation
*Ahead of time.* Write *i* and *I* on the board.
*Class time.* Review the formation of *i*, emphasizing its beginning point. Point out that the capital *I* is also begun with a straight downstroke, but it is taller.

### Teaching
Have pupils turn to page 62 and locate the picture at the top of the page. Read the sentences for pupils. Indicate that *Ivan* is a name and also the first word in a sentence, so capital *I* must be used. Point out that *I* in the second sentence is a word by itself. Emphasize that the word *I* is used when someone is talking about oneself. Explain that it is always spelled with a capital letter, even if it is in the middle of a sentence.

Ask pupils to look at the parts of *I* as you give the following directions:
—Start at the top line; slant down to the bottom line. Make a small crossbar on the top line. Make a small crossbar on the bottom line.
  [Down. Cross top. Cross bottom.]

Repeat the directions as necessary while pupils trace and write *I* independently.

page 62

Call attention to the incomplete sentence *I am a* _____ and the two pictures of a boy and a girl on the right. Explain to pupils that they should trace the words *I am a*, then write *girl* or *boy* from the print beneath the pictures. Instruct pupils to write the completed sentence below the traced sentence.

Discuss the next two sentences, pointing out that pupils must make a choice in the last one. Provide individual assistance as pupils complete the page.

### Activity
*Tube and clothespin puppets.* Have pupils use a toilet tissue tube for the body and a Popsicle stick (taped on the inside of the tube) for the handle. Pupils can decorate the tube puppet by adding face, arms, clothes, and so on.

Children may decorate a wood clothespin with scraps of paper and cloth. Pupils may draw on a face and add yarn for the hair. Have pupils identify each puppet by writing a specific letter on the puppet.

## Lesson 2, page 63

### Objectives

• Traces and writes manuscript letters *L* and *T* and sentences that contain *L* and *T*.

### Teaching

Have pupils turn to page 63 and locate the box at the top containing *l* and *L*. Point out that both *l* and *L* are the same height. Ask pupils to look at the parts of *L* as you give the following directions:
—Start at the top line; slant down to the bottom line; make a bar to the right.
[High start, down and over right.]

Repeat the directions as necessary while pupils trace and write *L* on the first two writing lines.

Call attention to the box containing *t* and *T*. Observe likenesses and differences between the two letters. Ask pupils to look at the parts of *T* as you give the following directions:
—Start at the top line; slant down to the bottom line. Make a crossbar on the top line.
[High start, down. Cross.]

Have pupils trace and write the letter independently. Repeat the directions as necessary.

Read the sentence near the middle of the page. Point out that capital *L* is used both at the beginning and within the sentence. Explain that *Louisiana* is the name of a state and must begin with a capital letter. Ask students to trace and write the sentence. After you have read the last sentence, explain that pupils will write the sentence by looking at the print.

Point out that most of the letters can be found elsewhere on the page if they need models. (The letter *r* is not found on the page.) If some children have difficulty writing from printed copy, provide individual assistance.

### Activity

*Letter-formation practice.* From time to time, give children the opportunity to practice writing letters they have learned. You might introduce the letters that are being reviewed on the chalkboard. When children have finished, go over their work with them. For individuals who need practice, select one or two letters to put on transparency film. Try to match the individual's natural writing size and slant to provide a model for his or her personal use. Instruct children to hold their film models over their writing to evaluate their letter formation. This type of activity will help children see the specific things they need to correct in their letter formation.

name _____

*L*   *L L L L L*   *L*

*L*

*T*   *T T T T T*   *T*

*T*

Linda lives in Louisiana.

*Linda lives in Louisiana.*

Trent lives in Tennessee.

page 63

## Lesson 3, preparation for page 64

### Objective
- Classifies others by physical features and similarities in clothing.

### Teaching, preparation for page 64

*Class time.* Ask one group of students to come up to the front of the classroom. Then guide the other pupils in classifying the students at the front by physical features, such as eye color, hair color, height, freckles, and so on.

Let a volunteer write two group characteristics on the chalkboard (*blue eyes* and *brown eyes*, for example). As students classify the groups at the front of the room, have children stand beside the appropriate label on the board.

Give several groups a chance to be classified at the front of the room. Also let several children have practice writing labels on the board.

You may vary this activity by having pupils classify others by the clothing they are wearing (*red shirts* and *blue shirts*, for example).

## Lesson 4, page 64

### Objectives
- Classifies pictured animals by physical features.
- Writes name of an animal below appropriate heading (spots, stripes).

### Teaching

Have pupils turn to page 64. As you discuss the characteristics of each pictured animal, bring out whether the animal has spots or stripes. Read each name and have pupils trace the writing. Point out that each label is a name; therefore, each word in the name begins with a capital letter.

Call attention to the label *stripes* on the left and *spots* on the right. Explain to pupils that they are

page 64

to write the name of each animal under the correct label. You may need to guide pupils as they begin by saying something similar to the following:

—Would you write *Lana Leopard* under *spots* or *stripes?*

Continue with individual guidance such as this if necessary.

### Activity

*Classification.* Provide experiences classifying objects in the classroom. You may start with things that are round or square. Gradually make these exercises more sophisticated by including extra criteria, such as things that are round and yellow, round and green, square and yellow, and so on.

# SECTION 18

**Pages 65, 66, 67**

Lesson 1, page 65
Lesson 2, page 66
Lesson 3, page 67
Lesson 4, review and evaluation

## Lesson 1, page 65

### Objective

• Traces and writes manuscript letters *J* and *U* and a phrase and sentence that contain *J* and *U*.

### Preparation

*Ahead of time.* Write *j*, *J*, *u*, and *U* on the chalkboard.

*Class time.* Review the formation of *j* and *u*. Point out that they both start near the middle line, but the capital *J* and *U* begin at the top line.

### Teaching

Have pupils turn to page 65 and locate the box near the top of the page containing *j* and *J*. Note the likenesses and differences between the two letters. Be sure to point out that capital *J* does not have a dot. Ask pupils to look at the parts of the letter *J* as you give the following directions:
—Start at the top line; slant down to the bottom line; curve left and stop.
[High start, down, and curve up left.]

Repeat the directions as necessary while pupils trace and write *J* on the first two writing lines. Emphasize the starting point at the top line.

Call attention to the box containing *u* and *U*, noting the likenesses and differences between the two. Ask pupils to look at the parts of the letter *U* as you give the following directions:

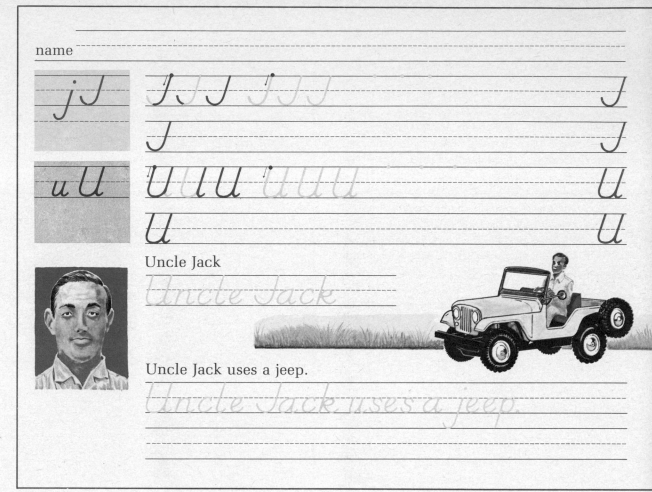

page 65

—Start at the top line; slant down to the bottom line; curve right; slant up to the top line; retrace down, and swing up.
[High start, down, over, up high, down, and a monkey tail.]

Repeat directions as necessary while pupils trace and write *U*. Emphasize the beginning point at the top line.

Have pupils look at the picture and trace the label *Uncle Jack*. Note that capital letters are used at the beginning of each word because both words are part of his name. Discuss the next picture and read the sentence for pupils. Tell pupils to trace the sentence, then write it independently. Point out that they will use the capitals *U* and *J* and the lower-case letters *u* and *j*. Emphasize correct letter formation, spacing, and the period at the end of the sentence.

# Lesson 2, page 66

### Objectives
- Traces and writes manuscript letters *H* and *K*.
- Writes a name below appropriate heading by matching the first letter of the name (*K* or *H*) to the first letter of the heading *(Kickball* or *Hopscotch).*

### Preparation
*Class time.* Review the formation of the letters *h* and *k* on the chalkboard.

### Teaching
Have pupils turn to page 66 and locate the box near the top of the page containing *h* and *H*. Note that they are the lower-case and capital forms of the same letter. Ask pupils to look at the parts of the letter *H* as you give the following directions:
—Start at the top line; slant down to the bottom line. Start at the top line, to the right of the first start; slant down to the bottom line. Make a crossbar on the middle line.
[High start, down. High start, down. Middle bar across.]

Have pupils trace and write the letter *H*.
Point out the box containing *k* and *K*. Give the oral directions for *K* as pupils study the models of the letter:
—Start at the top line; slant down to the bottom line. Start at the top line, to the right of the first start; slant left down to the middle line, and join; slant right down to the bottom line, and swing up.
[High start, down. High start, slant halfway, slant down, and a monkey tail.]

Repeat the directions as necessary while pupils trace and write *K*.

Call attention to the line of lower-case letters near the middle of the page. Point out that these are the letters they will need to use while completing this page.

page 66

Introduce the names of the four people pictured on the page. Ask pupils which begin with the letter *K* (*Kent* and *Kiku*) and which begin with the letter *H* (*Helen* and *Henry*). Point out the labels *Kickball* and *Hopscotch*, and ask pupils to tell you the beginning letter of each.

Tell pupils that the people whose names begin with *K* play the game that begins with *K*, and the people whose names begin with *H* play the game that has a name beginning with the same letter. Instruct pupils to write the names of the people under the correct headings (under *Kickball*, *Kent* and *Kiku*; under *Hopscotch*, *Helen* and *Henry*).

To provide some initial guidance, you might ask questions such as the following:
—Does Kent play kickball or hopscotch?
—Does *Kent* begin like *Kickball* or *Hopscotch?*

If necessary, continue with this type of guidance on an individual basis. Allow those who can to continue independently.

## Lesson 3, page 67

### Objectives
- Writes first letter of a given name.
- Develops concept that the first letter of a name can be used as an initial.

### Preparation
*Class time.* Review the formation of the letters H, I, J, K, L, T, and U.

### Teaching

Have pupils turn to page 67 and identify each letter on the second writing line.

Call attention to and identify the people pictured on the page. Tell students to write the first letter of each person's name on the writing space. If necessary, ask students to tell you which letter would be written for Tamika *(T)*. Instruct pupils to continue independently. Provide assistance for those who need it.

When everyone has finished, review the letter that should be written for each person. Explain to pupils that the first letter of a person's name is called an *initial*. Review this concept by asking questions such as the following:
—What is Jan's initial? Kevin's initial?

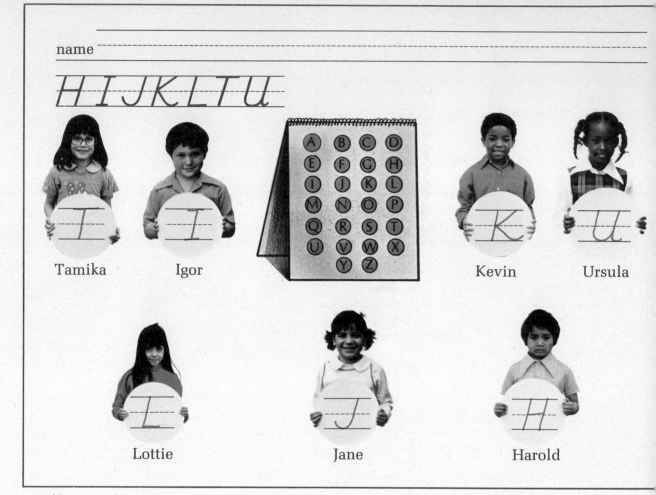

page 67

## Lesson 4, review and evaluation

### Objectives
- Writes first letter of a given name.
- Develops concept that the first letter of a name can be used as an initial.

### Preparation
*Ahead of time.* Choose students from your class whose first initials are any of the capital letters learned thus far: C, G, O, Q, S, H, I, J, K, L, T, or U. Write the capital letters on the chalkboard to serve as models. Supply writing paper for children.
*Class time.* Distribute the writing paper.

### Teaching, review
Ask three students, whose first initials are known capital letters, to come to the board and write their names. Have pupils number their papers and write the first initial of each name on their papers. Emphasize correct letter formation. Remind students that an initial must always be a capital letter. Continue in this manner with each group of three children having appropriate first initials. When the class has written the initials, review the correct initials on the chalkboard.

# SECTION 19

**Pages 68, 69, 70**

Lesson 1, page 68
Lesson 2, page 69
Lesson 3, page 70
Lesson 4, review

## Lesson 1, page 68

### Objectives
- Traces and writes manuscript letter *A*.
- Writes above a picture the sign that indicates the appropriate activity.

### Teaching

Have pupils turn to page 68 and locate the box containing *a* and *A* near the top of the page. Review the formation of *a* and introduce *A* as the capital form of the letter.

Ask pupils to look at the parts of the letter *A* as you give the following directions:

—Start at the top line; slant left down to the bottom line. Start at the same point on the top line; slant right down to the bottom line. Make a crossbar on the middle line.

[High start, slant left down. Same high start, slant right down. Cross.]

Emphasize that the cross stroke is written on the middle line. Repeat the directions as necessary while pupils trace and write the letter *A* on the first two lines.

Call attention to the lower-case letters. Tell pupils that these are the letters that they may refer to as they complete the page.

Discuss the pictures and labels below the lower-case letters. Bring out things pupils might see or do if they were to go to places like the ones pictured. Make sure children understand each label.

page 68

Instruct pupils to look at the first picture at the bottom of the page. Ask:

—Where are the children in this picture? (at an aquarium)

Instruct children to write a sign saying *Aquarium* above the picture. Allow children to continue writing the name of each place above each picture. Provide assistance on an individual basis if necessary.

### Activity

*Signs.* Encourage children to think of places they have been to that have a sign at the door or gate. If the names of the suggested places are spelled with known capital letters, write them on the chalkboard. Give children a choice as to which sign they would like to write. Distribute paper and allow time for children to write and decorate their signs.

## Lesson 2, page 69

### Objectives
- Traces and writes manuscript letter *B*.
- Writes words and phrases that contain the letter *B*.

### Preparation
*Ahead of time.* Be prepared to review any of the letters on page 69.

### Teaching ▬▬▬▬▬▬

Have pupils turn to page 69 and locate the box near the top containing the letters *b* and *B*. Discuss the two letters, pointing out that *B* is very similar to *b*. The loops are on the same side in both letters. This observation may benefit those who reverse *b* and *d*.

Ask pupils to look at the parts of the *B* as you give the oral directions.

—Start at the top line; slant down to the bottom line; retrace up; go right around, down to the middle line, and close; go right around, down to the bottom line, and close.

[High start, down, up, around halfway, around again.]

Repeat the directions as necessary while pupils trace and write *B* on the lines.

Call attention to the capital and lower-case letters on the next line. Explain that pupils may refer to these letters as models while they complete the page.

Point out the sign that says *Beach* in the middle of the page. Tell students that the picture shows places where items may be purchased at this beach. Identify the names of these items with pupils.

Explain that pupils should write the name of each item they might like. Remind them to refer to the model letters above if they need help with letter formation.

Provide assistance to those students who need it. Most pupils should be able to proceed independently.

page 69

### Activity

*Letter B Zoo.* Suggest that children think of names for animals that would appear in a zoo where all animals have names that begin with the letter *B*. You might want to start them off with names such as *Betty Bee*, *Buster Beetle*, and so on. Write the names on the board. Then let each child draw one of the animals and write the animal's name on a sheet of drawing paper.

## Lesson 3, page 70

### Objectives
- Traces and writes manuscript letter *D*.
- Writes a title and sentences that contain *D*.
- Adjusts space for first run-over sentence.

### Teaching

Have pupils turn to page 70 and locate the box containing *d* and *D* at the top. Review the formation of the letter *d,* and explain that *D* is the capital form of that letter.

Ask pupils to look at the parts of the letter *D* as you give the following directions:

—Start at the top line; slant down to the bottom line; retrace up; curve right around, down to the bottom line, and close.

[High start  down, up, around, and close.]

Repeat the directions as pupils begin to trace *D* and, if necessary, as they practice writing *D* on the writing lines.

Call attention to the picture of Doctor Dodge. Explain that *D* in *Doctor* is capitalized because *Doctor* is her title.

Read the sentence. Note with pupils that the *d* in *dentist* is not a capital within the sentence because it is not part of her title. Instruct pupils to trace the sentence, pointing out that it takes more than one line to write. Tell pupils to write the sentence on their own, using two lines and placing words just as they did when they traced the sentence.

Read the last sentence and ask pupils who is referred to by the word *She* (Doctor Dodge). Direct pupils to trace and write the sentence independently, paying close attention to letter formation and spacing.

### Special Populations

Children with learning problems have trouble remembering which direction the letters *B, b, D,* and *d* should face. Capital *B* is remembered as having two humps on the side, while *D* has one hump. Lower-case *b* and *d* are very difficult to remember. In addition to emphasizing different starting points, you need to teach these children a physical memory technique for recalling *b* and *d*. Have the pupils make their hands into fists with each thumb pointing up. Help them imagine that the fleshy bulge beneath each thumb represents the round part of *b* or *d*. The left thumb stands for *b,* and the right thumb stands for *d*. On the chalkboard, write *bed* as a cue word.

By memorizing hand signals, children can remind themselves which way *b* and *d* face.

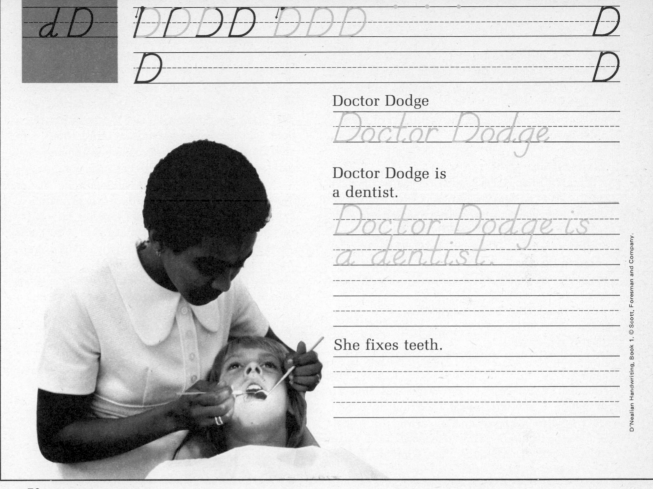

page 70

Doctor Dodge

Doctor Dodge is
a dentist.

She fixes teeth.

D'Nealian Handwriting, Book 1. © Scott, Foresman and Company.

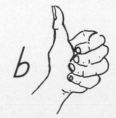

# Lesson 4, Review

## Objectives
- Reviews selected lower-case and capital letters.
- Reinforces concept that a capital letters is used as the first letter of the name of a public building or a street.
- Reinforces concept that the first letter of a name can be used as an initial.

## Preparation
*Ahead of time.* Have handwriting paper for each pupil. Select names of places pupils are familiar with that contain capital letters they have learned. *City Hall, Library,* and certain streets and avenues are some possibilities. If children have learned the capital letters in the name of their school, you might include that. Choose pupils' names containing known capital letters.

*Class time.* Distribute writing paper.

## Teaching, review
Tell children that they are going to learn to write names of places in their city or town. As you present the name of each place on the chalkboard, review the formation of letters—especially the capitals. Have children write the name on their paper.

Write the names of pupils you chose. Have children write the names, then underline the initials. If necessary, remind them that the first letter in each name is also an initial. If children seem to grasp this concept easily, you might include first and last names, asking pupils for two initials.

## Activity
*Letters come in all shapes and sizes.* Children may need to be reminded that letters do not always look the same. Demonstrate this to them by finding large examples of the same letter in several different type faces. Give children the opportunity to do the same thing. Provide them with magazines, scissors, paste, and paper. Let them volunteer for the letter they will look for. Encourage selection of varied letters, but caution children against selecting low-frequency letters, such as *Q.* If more than one child volunteers for the same letter, ask if the children would like to work together. Explain that they may search for both the lower-case and capital forms of their selected letter. When they cut out each letter, have them paste it on their paper. Advise children that the most varied type faces may be found in titles and ads. Display the completed collections of letters in alphabetical order.

# SECTION 20

**Pages 71, 72, 73**

**Lesson 1, page 71**
**Lesson 2, page 72**
**Lesson 3, page 73**
**Lesson 4, review and evaluation**

## Lesson 1, page 71

### Objective
• Traces and writes manuscript letter *M* and forms of address that contain *M* (*Ms., Mrs., Mr., Miss*).

### Preparation
*Class time.* Review formation of the letter *m*.

### Teaching
   Have pupils turn to page 71 and locate the box containing *m* and *M*. Introduce *M* as the capital letter form. Call attention to the models showing the steps to write *M*. The directions are:

—Start at the top line; slant down to the bottom line. Start at the same point on the top line; slant right, down to the middle line; slant right, up to the top line; slant down to the bottom line.
[High start, down. Same high start, slant down halfway, slant up, down.]

   Repeat the directions as pupils begin to trace and write *M* on the first two writing lines.
   Call attention to each person in the picture and discuss each label individually. Indicate that each form of address can be considered part of a person's name. Therefore, each should be written with a capital *M*. As you proceed, have pupils trace and write the names. Emphasize the period following *Ms., Mrs.,* and *Mr.* Tell pupils to concentrate on letter formation and spacing.

page 71

### Activity
   *Forms of address.* Now that children have been introduced to various forms of address, they will be eager to write names of people they know. Provide an opportunity for children to write the names of the principal, the librarian, other teachers, their parents, and other adults they suggest. Make sure they know all the capital letters in each name. Present each name on the chalkboard, emphasizing the formation of capital letters and the need for periods following the forms of address *Ms., Mrs.,* and *Mr.*

# Lesson 2, page 72

## Objective
• Writes number (1–10) that shows how many items are in each row of a bar graph.

## Preparation

*Ahead of time.* Collect simple bar graphs from posters, newspapers, and magazines, so that pupils may examine a variety of these graphs. You may find some bar graphs in your mathematics book.

*Class time.* Display the bar graphs, explaining that graphs such as these show how many items are counted in each part of a collection or survey. You might explain that children could make a bar graph of candy in a trick-or-treat bag on Halloween. Demonstrate on the chalkboard, using the same format as that found in the pupil book. The bar graph might look like this before you fill it in:

| | 1 | 2 | 3 | 4 | 5 | 6 | 7 | 8 | 9 | 10 |
|---|---|---|---|---|---|---|---|---|---|---|
| bubble gum | | | | | | | | | | |
| peanuts | | | | | | | | | | |
| apples | | | | | | | | | | |
| popcorn balls | | | | | | | | | | |
| licorice | | | | | | | | | | |

Ask volunteers to tell you how many pieces of each treat to put on the bar graph. Have children count as you fill in each section of a row.

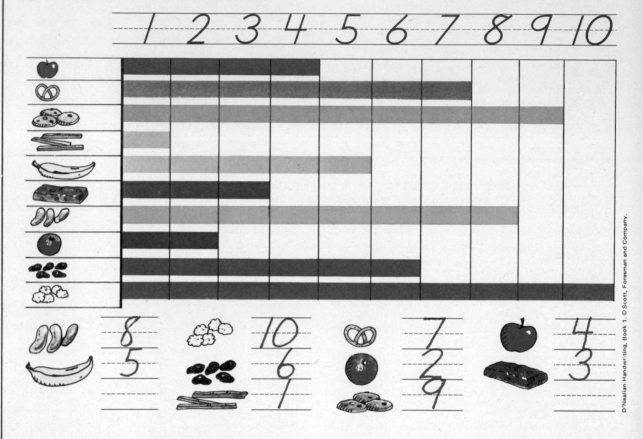

Elmwood School's Favorite Snacks

page 72

## Teaching

Have pupils turn to page 72. Read the title of the bar graph to pupils. If necessary, point out the numbers along the top and identify the items down the side of the graph (apple, pretzel, cookies, carrot sticks, banana, candy, peanuts, orange, raisins, popcorn). Point out the pictured items below the graph. Tell pupils that they should find the same item on the bar graph, count the number of colored spaces, and write the number next to the correct item at the bottom of the page.

To provide guidance, call attention to the picture of the peanuts below the graph and say:
—Find the peanuts on the graph, and tell me how many spaces are colored. [8]
—This means that eight people said peanuts were their favorite snacks. Write the number 8 next to the picture of peanuts below.

Continue with this type of guidance until it is no longer necessary.

## Lesson 3, page 73

**Objective**
- Writes a list.

**Preparation**

*Ahead of time.* Have on hand a supermarket ad from the newspaper.

*Class time.* Display the ad, pointing out various things that are advertised as a special. Ask how many students have seen their parents look through ads like this to make their grocery list. Tell pupils that they are going to look at some grocery lists other people have made. Then they will make one of their own.

**Teaching** ▬▬▬▬

Have children turn to page 73. Discuss Todd's and Bev's grocery lists, identifying the number and kind of items on each list.

Tell pupils that some items they might put on their lists are pictured. Call attention to the heading *My Grocery List*. Instruct pupils to write on the writing lines how many and what items they plan to buy at the store. Tell them that they may use items from the two lists on the page. More accelerated students may wish to add items that are not on the page. If necessary, help them with the spelling of these items by writing the words on the board.

Emphasize correct number and letter formation.

**Activity**

*I wish.* Indicate to children that people make other kinds of lists besides grocery lists. Tell them that they will have a chance to make another kind of list. Ask pupils to think of things they would like if they could have anything they could wish for. The lists may include tangible things (such as toys or a pet) or less tangible things (such as a trip to the moon).

This activity serves a double purpose in that many of the items children will list may be brought up again in the next lesson. This introduction, ahead of time, will expedite selection of the toys and games to be included on the graph.

name

Todd's Grocery List
3 carrots
7 oranges
eggs

Bev's Grocery List
2 pies
cereal
milk
10 apples

CEREAL    MILK

*My Grocery List*

73

page 73

# Lesson 4, review and evaluation

## Objectives
- Writes a form of address that contains *M (Ms., Mrs., Mr.,* or *Miss).*
- Writes number (0-10) and item that show how many are in each row of a bar graph.
- Writes a list.

## Preparation
*Ahead of time.* Draw the skeleton of a bar graph, such as the one on page 72 of the pupil's book on the chalkboard or on a transparency to be used on the overhead projector. Include only the numbers (0-10) along the top.

## Teaching, review and evaluation
Tell students that the class is going to graph their favorite toys and games. Explain that first they need a title for their graph. Suggest your name as part of the title. Ask a volunteer to tell what form of address *(Ms., Mrs., Mr.,* or *Miss)* should be used with your name. Then complete the title. It might read something like the following: *Ms. Brown's Class—Special Toys and Games.*

Ask volunteers to contribute names of toys and games for the graph. Explain that you will have to reject any games that are spelled with capital letters that the class has not learned yet. After the allotted number of spaces on the left are filled, tell pupils it is time to vote.

Ask pupils to raise their hands as you read the name of their favorite of those games and toys listed on the board. You may want to read through the list once before the voting begins.

As pupils vote for each item, fill in the correct number of spaces. If you should get more than ten votes for an item, explain that when the whole row is full, it can mean *ten or more.* As you fill in each space, have pupils count with you.

When the voting is complete and the graph is finished, pass out paper to each child. Instruct pupils to write their names on the paper and the title of the class bar graph. Tell them to make a list of the favorite toys and games and write how many votes each one got. You could provide initial guidance by listing the first item and number of votes on the chalkboard (for example, *checkers 2*).

Go over children's handwriting with them individually. Praise them for the elements they have done well (letter form, slant, size, and spacing). Give specific suggestions for improvement when necessary (the tail on *y* goes below the line, for example).

## Activities
*Bar graphs.* Ask children to look for more examples of bar graphs at home. After pupils have asked their parents if they may bring the bar graphs to school, allow them time to share them with the class. This experience will give children the idea that many things may be depicted on a bar graph.

*A list for all reasons.* Explain to children that there are many different kinds of lists. They have had exposure to a few—grocery lists, wish lists, and lists developed from bar graphs. Tell children to ask their parents what kinds of lists they make and use. Later, in a discussion, bring out different types of lists people use. Explain that pupils also use lists, such as a spelling list but may not realize it.

*Monograms.* When children have a reasonably good understanding of the concept that first letters of names may be used as initials, explain that a monogram is a person's initial or initials on an object. If possible, provide visual examples of things that are monogrammed. Explain that people have many things monogrammed, such as towels, clothing, dishes, glasses, stationery, and so on. Ask if their family owns anything that is monogrammed. Explain that monograms often are made with very fancy letters. Allow students time to design their own monogram on a piece of paper.

# SECTION 21

Pages 74, 75, 76

**Lesson 1**, page 74
**Lesson 2**, page 75
**Lesson 3**, page 76
**Lesson 4**, review and evaluation

## Lesson 1, page 74

### Objectives
- Traces and writes manuscript letter N.
- Develops concept that each word in a title begins with a capital letter.
- Writes a title and sentences that contain the letter N.

### Preparation
_Ahead of time._ Have on hand a front page from a newspaper.
_Class time._ Review formation of n.

### Teaching
Have pupils turn to page 74 and locate the box containing n and N at the top. Introduce the letter N as the capital form of n.

Ask pupils to look at the models of N. Give the following oral directions as they do so:

—Start at the top line; slant down to the bottom line. Start at the same point on the top line; slant right, down to the bottom line; go up to the top line.
[High start, down. Same high start, slant down, up.]

page 74

Repeat the directions as often as necessary while pupils trace and write the letter N.

Call attention to the headline _Neighborhood News_. Explain that this is a newspaper title. Point out that each word in the title begins with a capital letter. To reinforce this concept, display the front page of the newspaper you brought to class. Indicate that each word in the real newspaper title also begins with a capital letter.

Tell pupils to look back at the newspaper title in the pupils' book. Instruct them to use their best handwriting as they write _Neighborhood News_ on the writing line.

Discuss the picture and read the sentences with pupils. Explain that these are news items in the _Neighborhood News_. Tell pupils to concentrate on letter formation and spacing as they write the sentences.

Call attention to the printed label _My News_ and the writing line beneath it. Explain that pupils may write a sentence that tells some news about themselves or their families.

If children have difficulty thinking of some news, talk with the class for a few minutes, providing some possible topics.

Children may need help with spelling and sentence construction. Be available to write words on the chalkboard and to give individual guidance.

# Lesson 2, page 75

## Objectives
- Traces and writes manuscript letters *P* and *R* and names that contain *P* and *R*.
- Writes names in the order in which they appear along a pathway.

## Preparation
*Class time.* Review the formation of *p* and *r*.

## Teaching ▪▬▬▬▬▬▬

Have pupils turn to page 75 and locate the letters *p* and *P* at the top of the page. Note the similarities and differences between the lower-case and upper-case forms of the letter.

Call attention to the models showing parts of the letter *P* as you give the oral directions:

—Start at the top line; slant down to the bottom line; retrace up; go right around, down to the middle line, and close.

[High start, down, up, around, halfway, and close.]

Allow time for pupils to trace and write *P* on the writing lines.

Have pupils look at *r* and *R* in the box on the left. Introduce the capital *R*. Ask pupils to look at the models of the parts of the letter *R* to learn how to write it. The oral directions are:

—Start at the top line; slant down to the bottom line; retrace up; go right around, down to the middle line, and close; slant right down to the bottom line, and swing up.

[High start, down, up, around halfway, slant down, and a moneky tail.]

Repeat directions as necessary while pupils trace and write *R*'s on the two writing lines.

Explain that pupils will use the lower-case letters on the next writing line as they complete the page.

Call attention to the lower part of the page. Have pupils draw Pepper Rabbit's path to Radish Road

without touching a line. Then tell students to write on the numbered writing lines the names of the places in the order that they appear on the path. Explain that pupils should write neatly, concentrating on the capital letters and spacing. Remind them that they may check their lower-case letters with the models near the middle of the page.

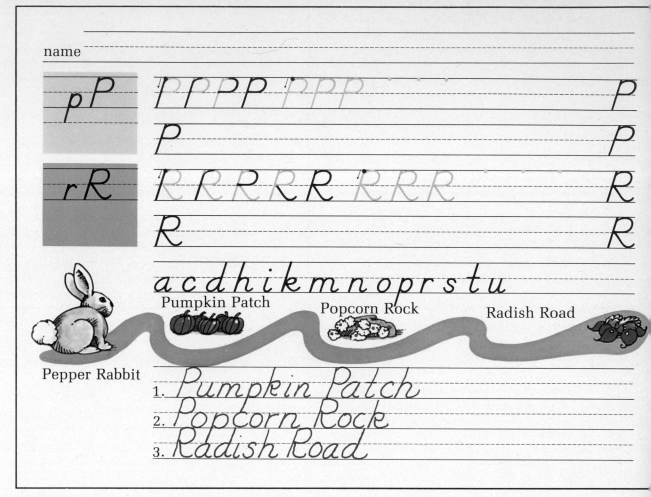

page 75

# Lesson 3, page 76

## Objectives
- Classifies pictured objects by color.
- Writes a name below appropriate heading (*red* or *green*).

106

## Teaching

Have pupils turn to page 76 and identify the letters at the top of the page. Review any that pose a problem for members of the class.

Call attention to the T-shirts and identify the name on each. Point out the headings *red* and *green* below the T-shirts. Have pupils write each name appearing on a red T-shirt under the heading *red* and each name on a green T-shirt under *green*.

Remind pupils to refer to the letters at the top of the page if necessary. Provide assistance to those who need it.

## Lesson 4, review and evaluation

### Objectives
- Classifies people.
- Writes names below an appropriate heading *(boys or girls)*.

### Preparation

*Ahead of time.* Prepare an alphabetical list of children in your classroom whose first names begin with the following letters: *A, B, D, M, N, P, R.* Include an equal number of girls and boys. You may put the list on the chalkboard or on chart paper. Have available handwriting paper for each child in the class.

*Class time.* Distribute the paper. Instruct pupils to fold their papers in half (perpendicular to the writing lines). Then have children open the paper and draw a line down the center of the page on the fold.

ABDMNPR abcdehilmnotvy

Nancy   Michelle   Paco   Amanda   Reva   Don   Anthony   Bob

red

Michelle
Paco
Reva
Anthony

green

Nancy
Amanda
Don
Bob

page 76

## Teaching, review and evaluation

Write the headings *Girls* and *Boys* on the chalkboard. Have pupils write the headings at the top of their columns.

If necessary, identify the names on your alphabetical list for the class.

Explain that pupils should write each name on the list under the appropriate heading. Circulate among students to provide individual assistance with procedure and letter formation.

When pupils have finished, review the names that should be in each column. Collect the papers to evaluate handwriting.

### Activity

*Architect.* Give two or three pupils pencils and sheets of construction paper. Then blindfold the children. Tell them that you will give them directions for things the children are to draw. The directions may be similar to the following:
—Draw a house.
—Then draw a garage beside the house.
—Draw a car in front of the garage.
When children have finished, take off their blindfolds and let them have fun admiring their silly drawings. Have children put their names on the papers and display them for the rest of the class.

# SECTION 22

## Lesson 1, page 77

### Objectives
- Traces and writes manuscript letter *E*.
- Writes safety signs that contain *E*.

### Teaching

Have children turn to page 77 and identify *e* and *E* in the box near the top of the page. Indicate that they are the lower-case and capital forms of the same letter.

Give the oral directions as pupils look at the models showing the steps for writing the letter *E*.

—Start at the top line; make a bar to the left on the top line; slant down to the bottom line; make a bar to the right. Start at the middle of the letter; make a bar to the right.

[High start, over left, down, over right. Middle bar across.]

Repeat the directions, emphasizing the beginning point, as pupils trace and write *E*.

Point out that the capital letters on the writing line are for pupils to refer to as they complete the page. Review any capital letters that are difficult for members of the class.

Call attention to and identify each sign pictured on the page. Discuss the meaning of each sign and possible locations where it might be found. Explain that often important signs such as these are printed with all capital letters. Tell pupils to choose three signs and copy them using their best handwriting. Emphasize that pupils should place the words on the writing lines just as they are shown on the signs.

page 77

### Activity

*Traffic and safety signs.* Give children paper and introduce other signs on the chalkboard, complete with shapes (octagonal *STOP* sign, for example). Let children practice writing the words on the sign, using the capital letters they know. Encourage them to draw the shape of the sign around the words. Other signs you might introduce are *CAUTION, NO PARKING,* and *NO U TURN.* Check the driver's manual for your state or just look around the city you live in for other signs using all capital letters.

## Lesson 2, page 78

### Objectives
- Traces and writes manuscript letter *F*.
- Writes words that contain *F*.

### Teaching ■

   Have children turn to page 78. Read the sign at the top of the page, and ask where pupils might see a sign like this. If necessary, point out that it might be found at a restaurant or community center.

   Call attention to the box at the left and introduce *F* as the capital form of the letter *f*. Ask pupils if they can point out the letter *F* in two places on the sign.

   As pupils study the parts of the letter *F*, give the following oral directions:

–Start at the top line; make a bar to the left on the
 top line; slant down to the bottom line. Start at the
 middle of the letter; make a bar to the right.
[High start, over left, down. Middle bar across.]

   Repeat the directions as necessary while pupils trace and write *F*.

   Discuss each picture and have pupils trace the labels. Explain that these foods should be on the menu at the right, but the printer forgot to put them in. Now the restaurant owner needs help. Ask children to write each food label on the menu to the right. Indicate that each item on the menu begins with a capital letter. Remind students that they must write neatly so that the customers can read the menu.

page 78

# Lesson 3, page 79

## Objective
• Traces and writes manuscript letter Z and words and sentences that contain Z.

## Teaching ▬▬▬▬▬

Have children turn to page 79 and locate the box containing z and Z. Note the similarities between the lower-case and capital forms of the letter. Explain that pupils will write both forms in this lesson.

Ask pupils to look at the models showing the parts of Z as you give the oral directions.
—Start at the top line; make a bar to the right on the top line; slant left down to the bottom line; make a bar to the right.
[Over right, slant left down, over right.]

As pupils begin to trace Z, repeat the directions. Allow students to continue practicing this new letter on the writing lines.

Discuss the picture and read the accompanying sentences. Note that the first sentence takes up two lines. Instruct pupils to trace each sentence, noticing the spacing between words. Explain that students should write the sentences on the blank writing lines, spacing the words just as they did when they traced the sentences.

## Special Populations

This will be a difficult lesson for pupils who reverse symbols. They usually turn the letter Z backwards. Pages 77 and 78 presented E and F beginning with a stroke to the left. On page 79 pupils must reverse direction, beginning Z with a stroke to the right. Mirror-image pupils and those who are confused by left and right will be especially frustrated in establishing the direction of Z. For these children, provide large cutout capital letters (E, F, and Z) that are the same color on both sides. Spend as much time as you can helping the children rehearse which direction the

page 79

letters should face. After the pupils feel confident with the cutout letters, have them practice writing on the chalkboard as you call out different letters. Then have them practice on clearly lined writing paper. In future lessons, be alert for continued problems involving the direction these letters should face.

## Activity

*Dictionary words.* Show children a page from a beginning dictionary, such as *Scott, Foresman Beginning Dictionary* (Scott, Foresman and Company, 1976). Point out how few words begin with the letter z. Read some of the more interesting words and let children write them. *Zebu, Zeppelin, zigzag, zinnia, Zip Code, zither, zoologist,* and *zoom* may interest children.

# Lesson 4, page 80

## Objectives
- Traces and writes manuscript letter *V* and sentences that contain *V*.
- Answers a question with a complete sentence.

## Teaching

Have pupils turn to page 80 and locate the model letters in the box at the top of the page. Note the similarities between the lower-case *v* and capital *V*.

Tell students to study the parts of the letter *V* as you give the following directions:

—Start at the top line; slant right down to the bottom line; slant right up to the top line.

[Slant right down; slant right up.]

Repeat the directions as pupils begin to trace and write *V*.

Discuss the pictures and read the sentences with pupils. Have pupils trace and write the sentences independently, noting spacing, letter formation, and use of capital letters.

Call attention to and discuss the printed question at the bottom of the page. Instruct pupils to answer the question with a complete sentence. If necessary, provide guidance by instructing them to begin their sentence with the words *I like*.

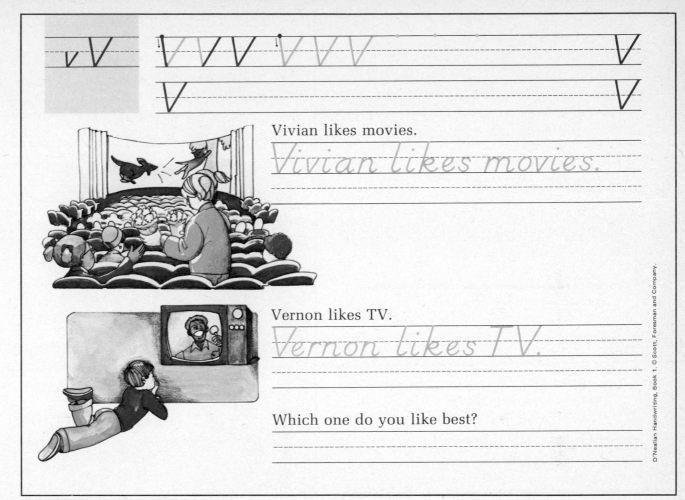

Vivian likes movies.

*Vivian likes movies.*

Vernon likes TV.

*Vernon likes TV.*

Which one do you like best?

D'Nealian Handwriting, Book 1. © Scott, Foresman and Company.

page 80

111

# SECTION 23

**Pages 81, 82, 83**

Lesson 1, page 81
Lesson 2, page 82
Lesson 3, page 83
Lesson 4, review

## Lesson 1, page 81

### Objectives
• Traces and writes manuscript letter *W*.
• Writes the answer to a question.

### Teaching

Instruct children to turn to page 81 and locate the models of the lower-case *w* and the capital *W*.

Ask pupils to study the four steps for writing the letter *W* as you give the oral directions.

—Start at the top line; slant right down to the bottom line; slant right up to the top line; slant right down to the bottom line; slant right up to the top line. [High start, slant right down, slant right up, slant right down, slant right up.]

Repeat the directions as necessary while pupils trace and write the letter *W*.

Identify the people in the pictures on the left side of the page, pointing out that these people will appear in other pictures on the page. Instruct pupils to trace the names.

Discuss each picture on the right and its accompanying question. Allow pupils time to answer the questions with one of the names they have just traced.

When everyone is finished, review the correct answers to the questions.

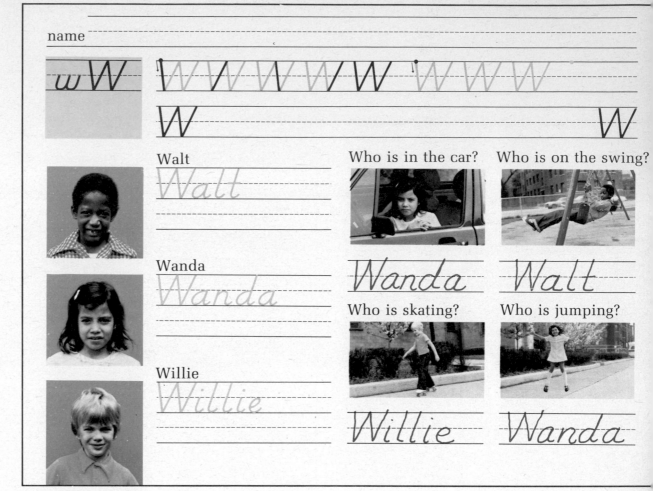

page 81

### Activity

*Seventeen fence posts.* On a worksheet or chalkboard, mark down seventeen parallel lines. Let children play the game in pairs.

The object of the game is to make one's opponent cross out the last post. Either child may start the game. Children may mark one, two, or three at a time, playing alternately. Pupils must figure out how to make the opponent cross out the last or final post.

## Lesson 2, page 82

### Objectives
- Writes the name of each day of the week.
- Develops the concept that the name of a day of the week begins with a capital letter.

### Preparation
*Ahead of time.* Have on hand a large calendar on which the names of the days of the week are clearly printed.

*Class time.* Display the calendar. Point out and identify the name of each day of the week. Indicate that each word begins with a capital letter.

### Teaching
Have pupils turn to page 82 and examine the calendar pictured there. Ask students if the names of the days of the week begin with lower-case letters or capitals. After someone gives the answer, explain that the names of the days of the week always begin with capital letters—no matter where they are found.

Tell pupils to write the appropriate day of the week on each writing line.

Point out that pupils may refer to the letters at the top of the page if they have difficulty recalling how to write a letter. Circulate among students, providing assistance with letter formation, if necessary.

### Activity
*Calendar.* If you do not already have and use a class calendar, now is a good time to start. At the beginning of each morning, discuss the date, weather, and important events that children should be aware of (for example, a school play that night, a field trip a day or two away for which some pupils still need to bring back permission notes, and so on). Have a volunteer come to the front of the class and write on the chalkboard the day of the week, the date, and maybe even a sentence about the weather, such as "Today is sunny."

page 82

## Lesson 3, page 83

### Objective

- Traces and writes manuscript letters *X* and *Y* and writes sentences that contain *X* and *Y*.

### Teaching ▬▬▬▬

Help pupils turn to page 83 and locate the box containing the models of the letters *X* and *x*. Point out the similarity between the two letters.

Ask pupils to look at the parts of the letter *X* as you give the oral directions.

—Start at the top line; slant right down to the bottom line, and swing up. Cross the letter with a slant left. [High start, slant right down, and a monkey tail. Cross.]

Have pupils look at the parts of the letter *Y* as you give the following directions:

—Start at the top line; slant right down to the middle line. Start at the top line, to the right of the first start; slant left down, join the first slant at the middle line, and go down to the bottom line. [High start, slant right halfway. High start, slant left down.]

Call attention to and discuss the picture on the right. Read the sentences and ask pupils who the word *He* refers to in the second sentence (Yoshio). Then ask what the word *them* in the same sentence refers to (X rays).

Instruct pupils to trace and write the sentences. Have them concentrate on letter formation, letter spacing, and a period at the end of each sentence.

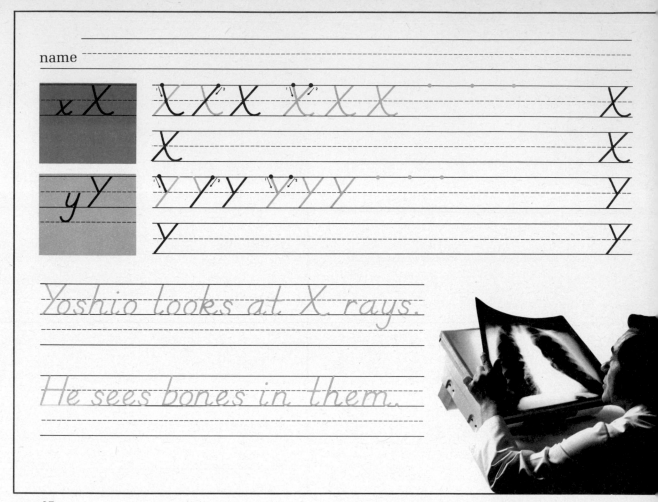

page 83

## Lesson 4, review

### Objectives

- Writes own first and last name using capital letters.
- Writes own address.
- Writes own telephone number.

### Preparation

*Class time.* Explain to children that they are going to make a class address book. Tell them they will need to practice writing their name, address, and telephone number correctly. Many children will already be able to write their address and telephone number. For those who cannot, write each for them on a sheet of paper. Allow time for them to practice.

### Teaching, review

Distribute paper and have children write and fill in the following:

I am _____ .
My address is _____ .
My telephone number is _____ .

Remind children that capital letters begin sentences, their names, and each word in the name of a street.

You may also wish to have children draw a picture of their house and family. When they have finished, put all the pages together in book form. Make a cover with a title, such as *Class Address Book.*

# SECTION 24

**Pages 84, 85, 86**

Lesson 1, page 84
Lesson 2, preparation for pages 85 and 86
Lesson 3, page 85
Lesson 4, page 86

## Lesson 1, page 84

### Objective
• Recognizes and writes correct form of lower-case manuscript letters *a, b, d, e, k, r, s, t.*

### Preparation
*Ahead of time.* Be prepared to review the formation of any lower-case manuscript letters.

### Teaching
Have pupils turn to page 84 and examine the letters on the top line of that page. Ask pupils what the letters on this line have in common (tall lower-case manuscript letters). Review similarities between these letters, including those that start at the top line *(b, h, k, l, t)*, near the top line *(f)*, and at the middle line *(d)*.

Call attention to the second row of small lower-case letters. Discuss common characteristics, such as which are made with straight lines *(v, w, and z)*, which letters begin with a curve to the left *(a, c, e, and o)*, and so on.

Ask pupils what the letters on the third line have in common (letters that go below the bottom line). Also ask what other similarities exist among some of these letters.

After sufficient review of the lower-case manuscript letters, call attention to each numbered line on which rests a correctly formed letter and an incorrectly formed letter. Tell pupils to circle the correctly formed letter as you give the oral directions. Then instruct them to carefully write it on their own.

page 84

D'Nealian Handwriting, Book 1. © Scott, Foresman and Company.

The oral directions for each manuscript letter are listed below.

s —Start a little below the middle line; go up to the middle line; go left around, down halfway; then go right around, down to the bottom line; curve left and stop.
[Curved start, around left, and a snake tail.]

a —Start at the middle line; go left around, down to the bottom line, around and up to the beginning; close; retrace down, and swing up.
[Around, down, up, down, and a monkey tail.]

r —Start at the middle line; slant down to the bottom line; retrace up; make a hump to the right, and stop.
[Down, up, and a roof.]

d —Start at the middle line; go left around, down to the bottom line, around up to the top line; retrace down, and swing up.
[Around, down, up high, down, and a monkey tail.]

115

k—Start at the top line; slant down to the bottom line; retrace up halfway; make a loop to the right and close; slant right to the bottom line, and swing up. [High start, down, up, small tummy, and a monkey tail.]

b—Start at the top line; slant down to the bottom line; go right around, up to the middle line; curve left and close.
[High start, down, around, up into a tummy.]

t—Start at the top line; slant down to the bottom line, and swing up. Make a crossbar on the middle line. [High start, down, and a monkey tail. Cross.]

e—Start between the middle and bottom lines; curve right up to the middle line; go left around, down to the bottom line; curve right and stop.
[Curve up, around, down, up, and stop.]

# Lesson 2, preparation for pages 85 and 86

## Objective
• Reviews lower-case and capital manuscript letters by matching pairs of letters.

## Teaching, preparation for pages 85 and 86

*Class time.* Ask pupils to turn to page 112. Have the children find the lower-case letter *c* and the capital letter *C*. Remind pupils that *C* was the first capital letter they learned. Note that the letters are similar and that it is easy to tell that *C* is the capital form and *c* is the lower-case form.

Tell pupils that they will be expected to write each matching pair of capital and lower-case letters.

If pages have not been torn out as pupils went along, you may prefer to have the class turn to page 55 and look at the letters *C* and *c* in the box. Then thumb through the book to page 81, talking about the letters in the boxes as you come to them.

# Lesson 3, page 85

## Objective

• Writes the lower-case manuscript letter equivalent to each given capital letter of the alphabet.

## Preparation

*Ahead of time.* Determine which of the children in your class are familiar with the matching pairs of lower-case and capital manuscript letters of the alphabet. They will be expected to write the lower-case form when given a capital letter. If you think some children in your class will be unsuccessful at this activity, provide them with the alternative instructions given at the end of the teaching below.

## Teaching

Have children turn to page 85. Explain that every capital letter of the alphabet may be found on this page. Remind pupils that for every capital letter, there is a lower-case form. Instruct them to write each lower-case manuscript form beside its matching capital letter. Point out that the pictures on the page are located by letters that begin the names of the pictures. Guide pupils in identifying each picture and pointing out which letter begins its name.

To provide initial guidance, identify the first capital letter as *A*, and ask pupils to write the matching lower-case letter on the writing line beside it. Continue with guidance of this type on an individual basis until no longer necessary. You may want to let children refer to page 112 as they work on this page.

*Alternative instructions.* Ask those children who would be unsuccessful at matching pairs of lower-case and capital manuscript letters to complete the page as follows. Instruct them to study each capital form on the page and, in their best handwriting, copy it on the writing line provided.

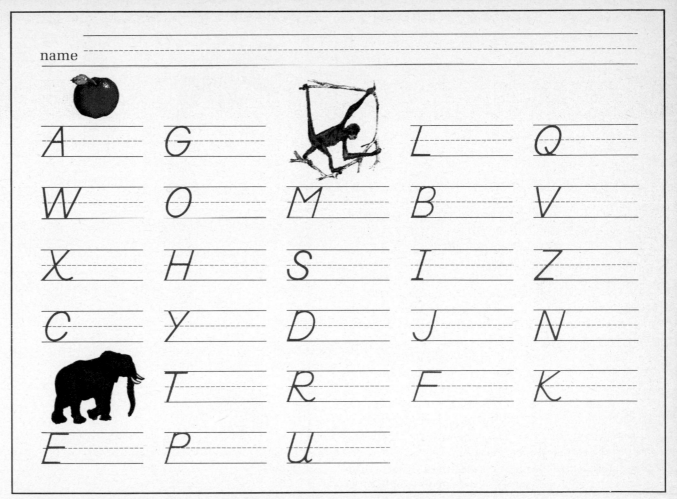

page 85

## Special Populations

This lesson lets you identify pupils still having trouble with direction of letters. Mirror-image pupils and those still confused by directionality cannot do this lesson well. Use this pupil page as an informal evaluation to pinpoint which capital/lower-case relationships are confused by various pupils. This information can help you refer certain children for special help.

# Lesson 4, page 86

### Objective

• Writes the capital manuscript letter equivalent to each given lower-case letter of the alphabet.

### Preparation

*Ahead of time.* Plan to use the alternative instructions below for children in your class who would not be successful in writing a capital manuscript letter when given a lower-case manuscript letter.

### Teaching ▬▬▬▬▬▬

Have children turn to page 86. Explain that every lower-case letter of the alphabet may be found on this page. Remind pupils that for every lower-case letter, there is a capital form. Instruct them to write each capital manuscript letter beside its matching lower-case letter. Point out that the pictures on the page are located by letters that begin the names of the pictures. Guide pupils in identifying each picture and pointing out which letter begins its name.

To provide initial guidance, identify the first lower-case letter as *b,* and ask pupils to write the capital form of the letter on the writing line beside it. Continue this type of guidance on an individual basis as long as necessary. You may want to let pupils refer to the alphabets on page 112.

*Alternative instructions.* Ask those children who would be unsuccessful at matching pairs of lower-case and capital manuscript letters to complete the page as follows. Instruct them to study each lower-case letter form on the page and, in their best handwriting, copy it on the writing line provided.

### Special Populations

Lessons 3 and 4 have shown you which pupils are too confused by directionality to succeed on their own. Provide sets of large cutout alphabets, both capital and lower-case forms. Make sure the color is the same on both sides. Different colors let some pupils memorize letter positions by color, not by correct direction. Teach the pupils to arrange capital

page 86

and lower-case alphabets separately in correct sequence with all letters turned the right way. When this is learned, have them combine corresponding capital and lower-case letters in alphabetical sequence until they can do so with no reversals. Next, have them write on the chalkboard, then on lined paper until they know the relationships and correct direction of all the letters. Children with true learning disability may not master this directional knowledge of the alphabet for several years.

# SECTION 25

**Pages 87, 88, 89, 90**

Lesson 1, page 87
Lesson 2, page 88
Lesson 3, page 89
Lesson 4, page 90

## Lesson 1, page 87

### Objectives
• Writes sentences and corrects errors in capitalization and punctuation.
• Writes a sentence that answers a question.

### Preparation
*Ahead of time.* Write on the board the name of any child in the class, using all lower-case letters. Then write a sentence using all lower-case letters and leaving out the period.

*Class time.* Identify what you have written on the board. Ask pupils what is wrong with the name (no capital at the beginning). Remind students that names almost always begin with a capital letter. Rewrite the name correctly. Read the sentence and guide pupils in locating the errors in capitalization and punctuation. Rewrite the sentence correctly.

### Teaching

Have pupils turn to page 87. Discuss each picture and read the accompanying sentence. Tell pupils to rewrite each sentence, correcting errors in capitalization and punctuation.

Call attention to the pictures across the bottom half of the page. Discuss the respective profession of each person. Point out that a man or a woman could hold any of these positions. Bring into the discussion the names of other possible careers. Write each job title on the chalkboard. Read the printed question below the pictures. Ask pupils to think for a minute

before they answer the question in a complete sentence. If necessary, provide assistance by telling pupils to begin their sentences with the words *I want to be.* Assist students with spelling if their career aspirations are not already on the chalkboard or the page.

### Activity
*Career awareness.* To promote awareness of various careers, you might invite some parents to come and

tell the class about their own vocations or avocations, such as musician, electrician, and so on. Don't overlook parents who perform volunteer services in the community, such as lecturers for museums, nurses' aides, and so on. If parents have equipment or pictures to display, the children will be all the more interested. Encourage parents to include information about times when their careers call for handwriting.

---

name

*melvin likes cars*
*Melvin likes cars.*
*he works hard*
*He works hard.*
*he wants to be a mechanic*
*He wants to be a mechanic.*

a doctor    a cook    a teacher    a barber    a writer

What do you want to be?

page 87

## Lesson 2, page 88

### Objectives
- Traces and writes a question mark.
- Writes a riddle and an answer.

### Teaching

Have pupils turn to page 88. Discuss the pictures and accompanying questions at the top of the page. Point out that each question ends with a question mark. Tell students that questions often begin with certain words. Have volunteers repeat the words beginning the questions at the top of the page. Encourage pupils to think of other words that are often used at the beginning of questions (*why, when,* and *what*).

Ask pupils to look at the models showing the formation of the question mark as you give the following directions:

—Start a little below the top line; make a part circle to the right, touching the middle line; slant down halfway to the bottom line, and stop. Add a dot on the bottom line.

Allow time for pupils to trace and write question marks on the writing line.

Call attention to the picture below the question marks. Read the riddle to pupils and discuss its meaning. Ask pupils to trace the question. Then have them write it exactly as they see it. Instruct pupils to trace *a monkey* and *a door key*, decide which is the answer to the riddle, then write only the answer on the line below the traced model.

Discuss the answer with pupils when everyone has finished.

page 88

D'Nealian Handwriting, Book 1. © Scott, Foresman and Company.

Riddle from *A Pack of Riddles* compiled by William R. Gerler. Text copyright © 1975 by William R. Gerler. Reprinted by permission of the publisher, E. P. Dutton and Co., Inc.

# Lesson 3, page 89

### Objective
• Writes a sentence that answers a riddle.

### Teaching
Have pupils turn to page 89 and identify the two animals pictured at the top of the page. Read the riddle with children and ask a volunteer to tell which animal is the answer (goose). Point out the manuscript sentence on the right, and explain that the answer is given here in a complete sentence. Note the capital at the beginning and the period at the end. Have pupils trace this sentence and write it independently on the writing line below.

Read the next riddle for pupils and point out the pictures and labels depicting the possible answers. Have pupils write a complete sentence, giving their choice of answers to the riddle. If necessary, explain that their sentence should begin, like the answer to the first riddle, with the words *I am a.*

Continue in this manner with the last riddle. When everyone has finished, review the correct answers to the riddles.

name

I am an animal.
My name begins with g.
What am I?

a goose    a dog

*I am a goose.*

I am an animal.
My name begins with t.
What am I?

a pig    a tiger

*I am a tiger.*

I am an insect.
My name begins with f.
What am I?

a fly    a bee

*I am a fly.*

page 89

## Lesson 4, page 90

### Objectives
- Copies a poem and its title.
- Develops concept that poetry has its own form.

### Teaching

Have pupils turn to page 90. Ask them to look at the poem "Pussy Feet" as you read it to them. When you have finished reading, ask pupils to point out the title. When someone indicates that *Pussy Feet* is the title, remind them that titles often have a capital letter at the beginning of each word.

Review the poem, pointing out that all poems are different, but that many begin each line with a capital letter, just as this one does.

Instruct pupils to write this poem just as they see it. Explain that each line should begin with the word containing the capital letter and that they should place the words on the lines exactly as they see them.

### Activity

*Cinquain.* This simplified form of cinquain ignores the requirement for a specific number of syllables. Pick a subject and compose the poem on the chalkboard with the class. They may then copy the poem on writing paper just as they see it on the chalkboard. This will reinforce the concept that a poem has its own form. A simplified cinquain form includes the following on each line.

Line 1: one noun
Line 2: two adjectives
Line 3: three verbs (*-ing* form)
Line 4: phrase with four or more words
Line 5: noun (can be repeated)

As you see, you will need to guide the class carefully, using the terms *describing words* and *action words* or *-ing words*.

Pussy Feet

My kitty makes
No noise because
She walks around
On velvet paws.

"Pussy Feet" by Ruth Chandler from *Child Life* magazine, copyright © 1967 by Review Publishing Company, Inc., Indianapolis, Indiana 46206.

page 90

Below is an example of this form of poetry.
    Snow
    Clean, white
    Sparkling, floating, landing
    Without so much as a sound
    Snow

# SECTION 26

**Pages 91, 92, 93, 94**

**Lesson 1, page 91**
**Lesson 2, page 92**
**Lesson 3, page 93**
**Lesson 4, page 94**

## Lesson 1, page 91

### Objective
• Writes a noun and adds *-es* to form plural.

### Preparation

*Class time.* Review with pupils that they already know we often add *-s* to words to make them mean more than one. Give pupils several examples on the chalkboard. Write *girl* and ask what they would do to make this word mean more than one girl (add *-s*). Write *boy* and ask what they would do to make it plural (add *-s*).

Indicate that some words need another ending to make them plural.

### Teaching ▬▬▬▬▬

Have pupils turn to page 91 and identify the first two pictures and labels (*bus* and *buses*). Ask pupils how the word *bus* was changed to make it mean more than one (*-es* was added).

Explain that *-es* is often added to words to make them plural, but usually only to words ending with certain letters. Point out that every word on this page must have *-es* added to it to make it mean more than one. Ask children to write the plural form of each word on the writing line provided. Circulate around the room, giving assistance where needed.

When everyone has finished, discuss the singular and plural forms of each word. Ask what letter the first word ends with (*s*). As you discuss each word, determine with pupils what letter or letters the word

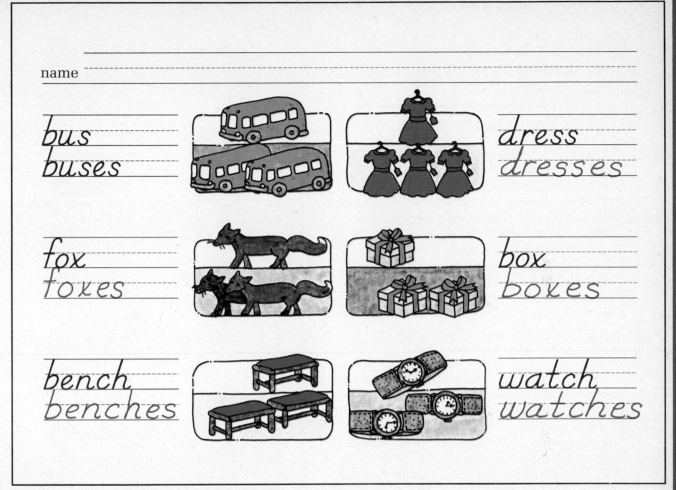

page 91

ends with. Explain to pupils that usually when words end with *s*, *x*, or *ch*, pupils will need to add *-es* to make them mean more than one. If necessary, ask students to underline the letters *s*, *x*, and *ch* at the end of the singular nouns.

## Lesson 2, page 92

**Objective**
• Writes words that show relationship between members of a family.

**Teaching**

Have children turn to page 92 and find the picture of Anna. Explain that the other people pictured on the page are members of Anna's family. Identify each person and that person's relationship to Anna.

Discuss whether pupils have as many relatives as Anna has. Ask if they have relatives other than the ones that Anna has. Some pupils may have foster parents or stepparents. If so, you will want to write the words representing their relationship on the chalkboard (*stepmother, foster father*, for example).

Call attention to the heading *My Family*. Instruct pupils to write the words representing their family members on the writing lines. Tell pupils to use their best handwriting.

**Activity**

*Tissue and wire designs.* Have pupils make designs using a piece of wire. Squeeze glue on the wire. Lay some tissue paper over this, and paint the tissue with a coat of glue. Lay other pieces of colored tissue on this and let them dry. Trim away the excess tissue. Paint both sides of the design with another coat of glue. Stand the designs in front of a window and let the light shine through it.

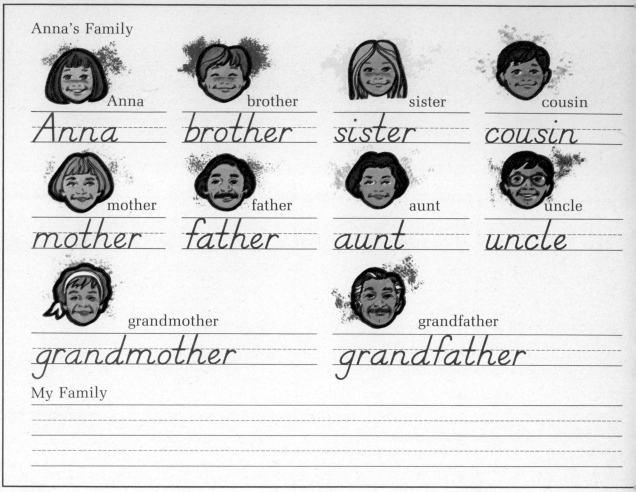

page 92

## Lesson 3, page 93

### Objective

• Traces and writes phrases that use an apostrophe to show possession.

### Teaching ▬▬▬

Have pupils turn to page 93 and look at the first three pictures on the page. Identify the label for each picture. Then have pupils trace *Tom's hat* on the writing line. Point out and identify the apostrophe. Note with pupils that the apostrophe begins with a little dot at the top line, then ends with a little tail. Tell pupils that it helps show that Tom owns the hat. Explain that an apostrophe and the letter *s* are added to names to show that the person named owns something. Usually the thing that is owned is named in the same phrase. Point out the next three pictures and labels. Ask What Mary owns (wagon). Point out the apostrophe and the letter *s* added to Mary's name. Then have pupils trace *Mary's wagon*.

If necessary, guide pupils through the next sets of pictures, instructing them to trace and write the phrases.

### Activity

*Labeling.* Provide practice for children in the use of the apostrophe to show possession. Plan on having them label things in the classroom that are theirs. Cut and distribute tagboard or blank sentence strips the size of a name tag on a desk. Instruct children to write their own name followed by *'s* and the word *desk*. Put the new labels on the appropriate desks. You could extend this activity if children have lockers, art boxes, mailboxes, or anything else that can be labeled.

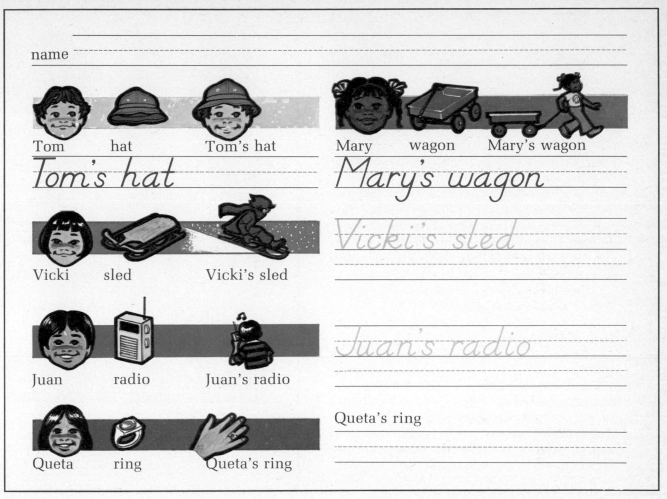

name

Tom    hat    Tom's hat    Mary    wagon    Mary's wagon

*Tom's hat*    *Mary's wagon*

Vicki    sled    Vicki's sled    *Vicki's sled*

Juan    radio    Juan's radio    *Juan's radio*

Queta    ring    Queta's ring    Queta's ring

page 93

125

## Lesson 4, page 94

### Objective
• Writes rhyming words and phrases.

### Teaching
Have pupils turn to page 94 and identify the first two pictures. Read *a wig* and *a pig*. Have pupils note that the ending sounds are the same. Explain that the words rhyme, and ask pupils to write each label. Call attention to the picture on the right and the accompanying label. Note that the phrase uses the rhyming words. Have pupils write the phrase.

Guide pupils in identifying the other pictures on the page. Instruct pupils to copy each label and then make up and write a rhyming phrase for each picture on the right.

Emphasize correct letter formation and spacing. Provide guidance where necessary.

### Special Populations
A specific learning disability generally called "tone deafness" (poor auditory perception) makes it impossible for certain pupils to do rhyming. They do not hear likenesses and differences in speech sounds. They cannot tell when words rhyme (sound alike). These children can learn to follow visual clues (spelling patterns) to find which words are alike or different, but they cannot do so through listening. Tone-deaf children hear only beginning consonant sounds. Sometimes they can identify ending consonants. Seldom do they hear middle sounds in words.

### Activities
*Rhyming words.* Children will gain an added appreciation of rhyming words in comical phrases and sentences as you read them the following book:

> *Did You Ever See?* by Walter Einsel (Reading, Mass.: Young Scott Books, Addison-Wesley, 1962).

After you read the book to children, you might ask if they can create and write their own "Did you ever see" rhymes.

page 94

*Auditory discrimination.* Provide a worksheet on which words are presented in groups of three. Two of the three words will rhyme. As you read the words, children will underline the two words that rhyme. You might wish to use the groups of words that follow:

| | | |
|---|---|---|
| 1. man | mat | tan |
| 2. fan | fat | cat |
| 3. sun | sat | fun |
| 4. fuss | fuse | bus |
| 5. torn | tear | born |
| 6. sad | last | lad |
| 7. fast | taste | last |

You might vary the activity by listing sets of rhyming words on the chalkboard in mixed-up order. Then have children pick out and write two words that rhyme.

# SECTION 27

**Pages 95, 96, 97, 98**

Lesson 1, page 95
Lesson 2, page 96
Lesson 3, page 97
Lesson 4, page 98

## Lesson 1, page 95

### Objectives
- Follows the order in which place names appear along a route on a map.
- Writes place names in sequence.

### Teaching

Tell pupils to turn to page 95 and identify the pictures and labels at the top of the page. Point out that the words in the name of each store begin with capital letters. Explain that the shoppers on this page will go to three of these places.

Review the formation of any letters that pose problems for children and explain that these letters will be used to complete the page.

Call attention to the shoppers on the page. Have children trace the track on the page, showing the places the shoppers will go. Point out that there is one place the shoppers will not go. Then instruct children to write the names of the places the shoppers will go in the order in which they visit them. Emphasize correct letter formation and spacing. Provide assistance for pupils who need it.

Remind pupils that they may refer to the letters above as they write the store names.

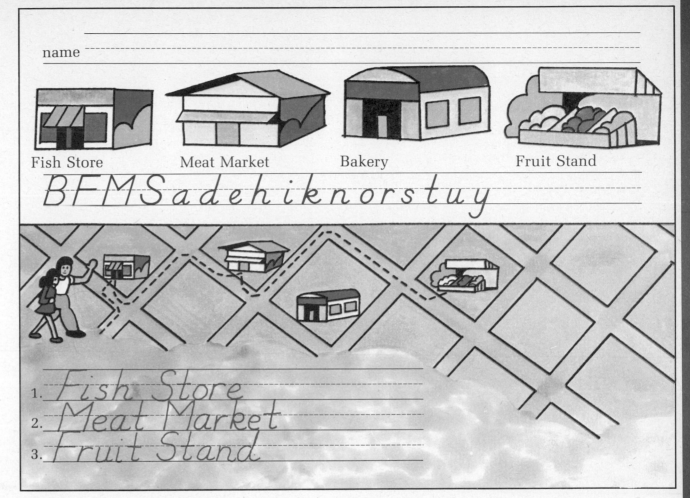

page 95

### Activity

*Alphabet Neighbors.* Let children play Alphabet Neighbors to become familiar with alphabetical sequence. Display the complete alphabet where children can easily see it. Let a volunteer write any letter on the chalkboard except *A* or *Z*. Then have another volunteer write one of that letter's alphabet neighbors —the letter that comes before it or after it in the alphabet. Continue the game with the class or let small groups play independently.

## Lesson 2, page 96

### Objectives
- Matches shapes to determine correct labels.
- Writes labels.

### Teaching

Tell children to turn to page 96 and study the letters at the top of the page. Explain that pupils will write these letters on the page.

Call attention to the picture and relate the following story to pupils.

—The Brown family went on a camping trip. When they went fishing, they left the food out in the open. It began to rain, and the labels started to wash off. The only way the Browns could tell what was in each container was to remember the shape of each and label the containers again.

Identify the containers near the top of the page. Have pupils match the shape of each container with one of the blank containers and write the appropriate label on the writing lines within the shape.

Emphasize correct letter formation. Remind children that they may refer to the model letters at the top of the page.

### Activity

_Word-shape match-up._ Explain to children that words have shapes. Indicate this by writing the words _dog_ and _pot_ on the chalkboard, along with the following shape.

Ask a volunteer to come to the board and write the word with the right shape in the blocks. Continue this activity by providing a larger selection of words along with a shape. Some suggestions follow:

| | | |
|---|---|---|
| boy | girl | go |
| mat | name | got |
| man | trip | game |
| map | sail | group |

You could continue this activity using reading vocabulary or spelling words.

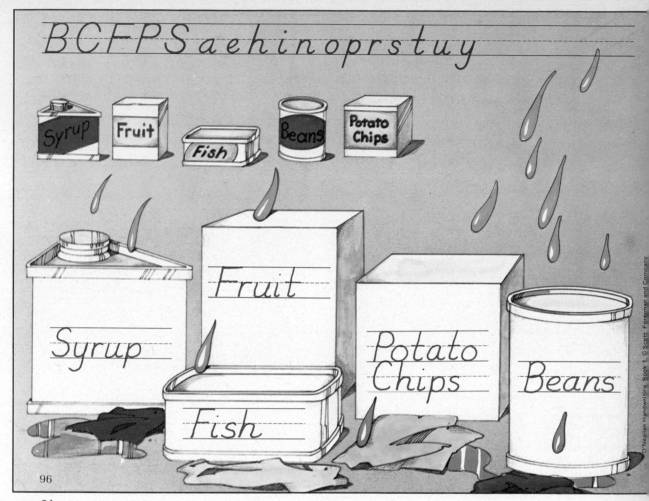

page 96

128

# Lesson 3, page 97

## Objectives
• Writes appropriate word(s) below a name by matching the beginning letter of each word (*A, a; C, c; D, d; H, h; M, m; P, p; R, r*).

## Teaching

Have pupils turn to page 97. Call attention to and identify the people pictured on the page. Ask pupils to identify the initial(s) of each person on the page. person on the page.

Tell pupils that all these people plan to go on a picnic and that each person is going to bring some food that begins with the same letter as his or her name (or initial).

Identify the food in the picnic basket and tell pupils to write the name of each food beneath the person's name beginning with the same letter. Note that pupils must match lower-case and capital letters.

If necessary, you may provide initial guidance such as the following:
—What food begins like Christopher's name? [carrots]
—What food is Christopher going to bring? [carrots]

If some children have difficulty, continue to provide assistance on an individual basis.

When everyone has finished, call attention to the question on the lid of the picnic box. Explain that pupils should write the name of a food that begins with the same letter as their first initial. Provide assistance with spelling.

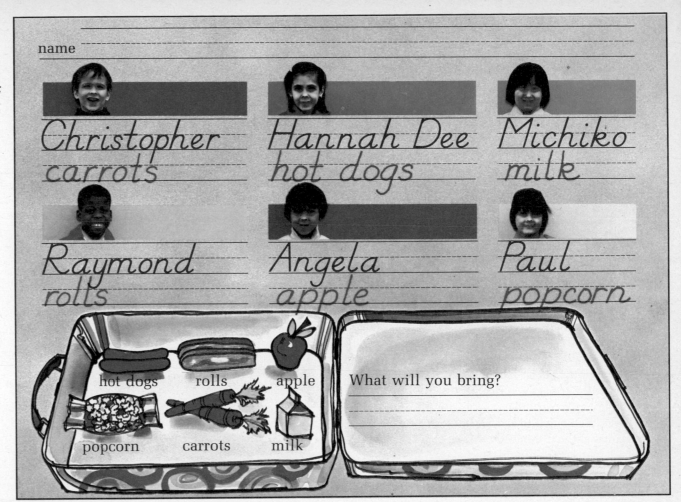

page 97

## Lesson 4, page 98

### Objectives
- Adjusts space when writing without lines.
- Writes a label.
- Draws an appropriate picture.

### Teaching

Have children turn to page 98. Identify the pictures and labels at the top of the page with pupils. Explain to pupils that each type of weather can be seen through one of the windows on the page. Call attention to the first window, and ask pupils to tell you what type of weather can be seen through the window (rainy). Point out that the sign next to the window has the word *rainy* and a picture of rain.

Tell pupils that they should look at the weather in each window, and choose the word describing the weather from the labels at the top of the page. Then instruct them to write the word on the sign next to the window and draw the picture of the weather that goes with the label.

This is the pupils' first experience in writing without writing lines. It is also the first time that D'Nealian models do not appear anywhere on the page. Tell pupils to concentrate on writing the letters as straight as if they were writing on a line. Emphasize correct letter formation and size.

When everyone has finished, review the labels on the signs. Have pupils evaluate their own writing without the aid of writing lines. Ask pupils if their handwriting improved from one sign to the next.

### Activity

*Writing practice without lines.* Provide children with a variety of experiences in writing without lines. You might provide instructions for writing on the chalkboard, the overhead projector, magic slates, or unlined paper. No matter what you have instructed children to write, make sure they concentrate on letter size and formation, as well as writing straight, as if a line were really there.

page 98

# SECTION 28

**Pages 99, 100, 101, 102**

Lesson 1, page 99
Lesson 2, page 100
Lesson 3, page 101
Lesson 4, page 102

## Lesson 1, page 99

### Objective
• Writes a phrase that uses correct position words *(in, above, over, behind)*.

### Teaching

Have pupils turn to page 99 and study the pictures at the top of the page. Discuss each picture and identify the word accompanying it, by asking where the bird is in relation to the umbrella. Use each label in a sentence, such as the following:

—The bird is *beside* the umbrella.

Point out that there are two words by the third picture. Introduce both words and indicate that they have the same meaning by using each in a sentence.

—The bird is *above* the umbrella.

—The bird is *over* the umbrella.

Direct attention to the question in the middle of the page. Ask pupils to look at the pictures below the question, and tell them to write a phrase using one of the position words above that tells where the bird is. Point out that the phrase that goes with the first picture has been written for pupils.

Have pupils use the position words at the top of the page as they write the phrases next to the remaining pictures independently. Emphasize correct letter formation and spacing. If necessary, provide assistance on an individual basis.

### Special Populations

Pupils with poor sensory integration will have diffi-

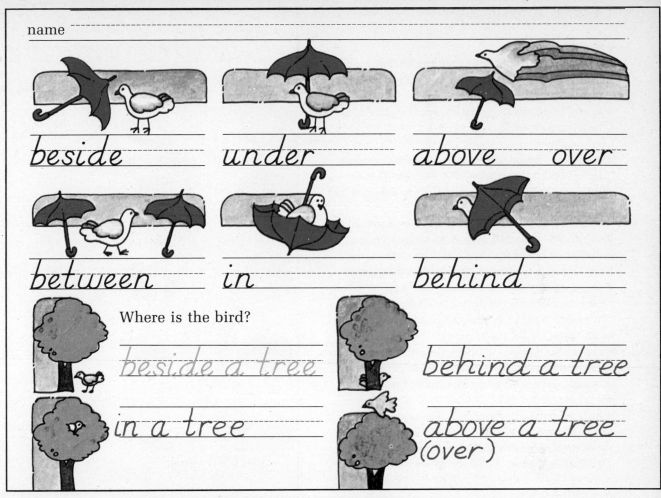

page 99

culty with the three terms starting with the letters *be: beside, between, behind*. Be alert for confusion with these terms and the concepts they represent. Provide multi-sensory practice for pupils who are confused by these concepts. Make flashcards of these words. Let pupils practice standing *beside* a desk, sitting *between* two friends, and hiding *behind* a bookshelf. Coordinate saying the terms, seeing them on cards, and doing what they say until the concepts make sense to your pupils.

### Activity

*Worksheets.* Make worksheets with a picture of something children are familiar with (a cloud, for example) drawn in the center. Then give instructions for children to draw objects or animals in, above, over, behind, beside, and under the cloud.

## Lesson 2, page 100

### Objectives

- Matches a pair of words that begin with the same letter (capital and lower-case) and draws a line between them.
- Writes sentences that contain words matched by beginning letters.

### Teaching

Have pupils turn to page 100. Indicate that the capital and lower-case letters at the top are ones that pupils will use to complete the page.

Call attention to the pictures and labels at the left. Tell children that they must draw a line to match names and objects that begin with the same letter. Point out that the names begin with capital letters and the objects begin with lower-case letters.

Have pupils trace the dotted line between *Quentin* and *quilts.* Read each label and point out that they begin with *Q* and *q,* two forms of the same letter. Read the sentence to the right, pointing out that both these words are in the sentence. Have pupils trace the sentence, noting letter formation, spacing, and the period at the end.

Instruct pupils to continue in the same manner, matching words beginning with the same letter and writing sentences in which those words are used.

Provide individual assistance where needed.

### Activities

*Concentration.* Make a small card for each lower-case and capital letter. Place the lower-case letter cards face down on the left and the capital letter cards face down on the right. Two pupils may play concentration by alternately turning over pairs of cards to find the lower-case and capital forms of the same letter. When players turn over a matched pair, they get to keep both cards and take another turn. The player with the most cards at the end is the winner.

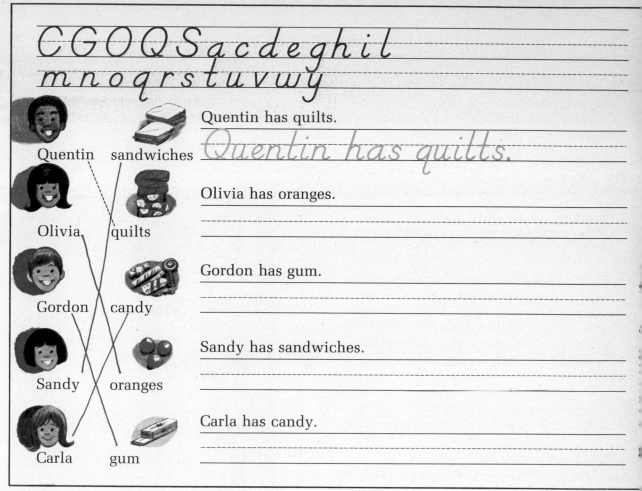

page 100

*Streetcar.* Choose one child to be the conductor. The child should stand behind the chair of the first child in the class. Flash a letter card (capital or lower-case). If the conductor can write the corresponding letter on the chalkboard, the conductor moves on to the next child. For example, if you flash a lower-case *h,* the conductor should write the capital *H.* If the child who was in the chair can write the corresponding letter on the chalkboard first, then that child has the next turn being the conductor.

# Lesson 3, page 101

## Objective
• Writes appropriate name to match pictures.

## Teaching

Have pupils turn to page 101 and examine the pictures at the top of the page. If necessary, identify the name of each person. Explain that all of these people are going to the same party. Point out that since they do not know one another, they will need name tags.

Tell pupils to write each person's name on the blank line next to his or her picture on the bottom half of the page. Emphasize neatness and correct letter formation, explaining that everyone should be able to read a name tag easily. Tell pupils that they may refer to page 112 to check correct letter formation. This is the second time pupils do not have a D'Nealian model on the page. Give extra assistance where needed.

Pupils should be able to complete the page independently. If necessary, you may provide initial guidance such as the following.
—Look at the first picture. Can you find the same person at the top of the page? That's right, April is her name. Write *April* neatly on the line.

Continue with this type of guidance on an individual basis until no longer necessary.

## Activity

*Creative writing center.* Your more accelerated students may enjoy being able to create and write stories independently. At a table in your classroom, provide paper, pencils, erasers, and a model of the D'Nealian alphabet.

Construct the word wheel described below and place it in the center. This beginning type of "dictionary" will serve to introduce new words and reinforce classification skills. To construct this word wheel, you will need tagboard, felt-tip pens, and a brad. Cut several half circles with a tab on each.

page 101

Write a category on each tab. Suggested categories are: *People, Animals, Numbers, Colors, Sizes, Feelings, Places, Doing.*

On each half circle, write words suggested by children or from reading books, social science lessons, and so on. Connect the half circles with a brad.

# Lesson 4, page 102

## Objectives
- Copies a poem.
- Develops concept that a poem has its own form.

## Teaching

Have pupils turn to page 102. Read the poem and discuss the picture. Make sure that pupils understand the meaning conveyed in the poem.

Reread the poem, and ask pupils if they hear any rhyming words. Point out that poems do not always need to rhyme. Indicate that some lines in the poem have only one word, while others have two or three. Tell pupils that the words in this poem will always be found on the lines they are on here. Indicate that this poem has its own form, and it should always look just the way it looks here.

Have pupils write the poem, placing words just as they see them on the lines of print. Indicate that each line begins with a capital letter. Emphasize that each line begins at the left, so that the beginning word of each line is lined up with the other beginning words.

Free
Is being able
To
Jump
Without falling.

"Free" by Ginger Allen from *Poetry in the Schools North Carolina* 1972 edited by Ardis Kimzey, Copyright © 1972 by North Carolina Department of Public Instruction. Reprinted by permission.

page 102

# SECTION 29

**Pages 103, 104, 105, 106**

Lesson 1, page 103
Lesson 2, page 104
Lesson 3, page 105
Lesson 4, page 106

## Lesson 1, page 103

### Objective
• Writes the lower-case letter equivalent to each given capital letter of the alphabet.

### Teaching

Have pupils turn to page 103 and identify the letters at the top of the page as all the lower-case manuscript letters of the alphabet.

Tell pupils that the capital letters of the alphabet are located below. Instruct them to write each lower-case letter beneath the capital form of the same letter. Tell pupils to take care in the formation of each letter, referring to the alphabet at the top of the page, if necessary.

You may provide initial guidance by having pupils identify the first capital letter (*O*) and asking them to write the lower-case manuscript form of the same letter beneath it.

Pupils should be able to complete this page independently.

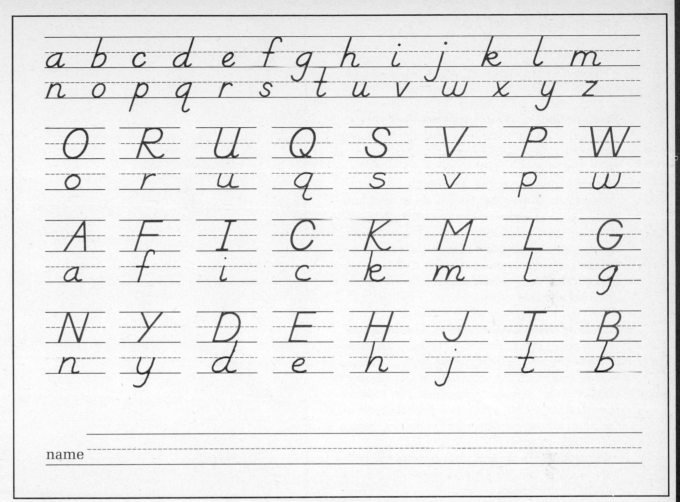

page 103

### Special Populations

Mirror-image pupils will reverse certain letters as they transfer from the top of the page to the lines beneath capital letters. Be alert for reversed direction and confusion in writing *b, d, g, j, p, q, s, y,* and *z.* Provide extra practice in writing these letters for the pupils who are confused by direction. Watch for backward strokes as pupils write the letters.

### Activity

*Individualized handwriting review.* Write a capital and the equivalent lower-case letter on a 4-inch by 6-inch card. Also write words containing that letter (again, capital and lower-case). Make one card for each letter of the alphabet. For durability, laminate each card or cover it with acetate.

Children may use these cards independently to practice letters that pose problems for them. Write a set of directions, such as the following, on the first card.

1. Copy each line 3 times.
2. Notice the slant, spacing, and how your letters are formed.

## Lesson 2, page 104

### Objective
• Writes the word *first*, *next*, or *last* below each picture in a set of three to show sequence.

### Preparation
*Ahead of time.* Choose three obviously sequential pictures showing a simple action. You may need to draw these pictures. An example of this might be an ice cube in different stages of melting.

*Class time.* Display the pictures out of sequential order. Ask a volunteer to identify which picture shows what happened first. At that point, introduce the word *first* by writing it beneath the picture or on the chalkboard and reading it aloud. Continue in this manner, identifying the sequential order of the pictures and introducing the words *next* and *last*.

### Teaching
Have pupils turn to page 104. Identify the three words at the top of the page *(first, next, and last)*. Explain that pupils will write these words beneath the pictures on the page to show the order in which they took place. Tell pupils that they may refer to the words at the top of the page for correct spelling and letter formation.

Call attention to the first three pictures and tell pupils to label each picture with one of the words to show the correct order.

Most pupils will be able to complete the page independently. To provide individual guidance, you might discuss the three pictures and ask the student to tell you which picture would have happened first. Have the student write *first*. Continue this step-by-step guidance until no longer necessary. Try to encourage everyone to complete labeling the last group of pictures independently.

### Special Populations
Pupils who have difficulty with this lesson need to work with moveable sequence objects. Provide sets of pictures, cutout comic strips, or actual objects that show various stages of change. Make flashcards with the words *first*, *next*, and *last*. Guide the pupils as they rehearse placing their objects under the correct label. This practice should include oral discussion of why each object should be placed in a given place within the sequence. Help pupils to observe minimal cues (minor details) that show evidence of first, next, or last. Encourage pupils to tell their reasons for deciding where an object should go within the sequence.

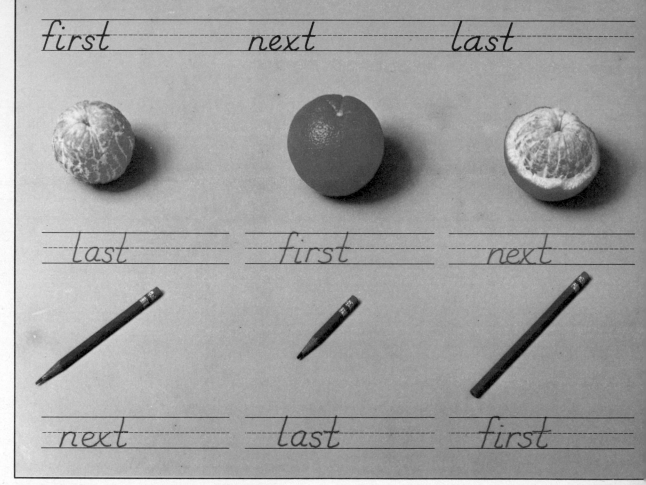

page 104

## Lesson 3, page 105

### Objectives
- Matches pictures.
- Writes words that have opposite meanings.

### Preparation
*Class time.* Remind students of experiences they have had in classifying objects. Review with them the words *hot* and *cold*, asking them to describe objects with each characteristic. Guide pupils toward making the generalization that *hot* is the opposite of *cold*. Continue the discussion with review of the words *big* and *little*, bringing out that these words, too, have opposite meanings.

### Teaching

Have pupils turn to page 105. Through discussion of the pictures and labels at the top of the page, guide pupils in determining which labels are opposites. If you wish, you may have pupils draw a line between the labels with opposite meanings.

Call attention to the pictures below. Indicate that pupils should label each pair of pictures with the two labels that have opposite meanings.

If necessary, discuss the first pair of pictures, asking which label would describe the face in the first picture *(happy)*. Have pupils trace the word *happy*. Then ask if the face in the second picture would be described with the same word or a different word *(different)*. Ask which word would describe this face *(sad)*. Have pupils trace the word *sad*.

Most pupils should be able to match the pictures and labels at the top of the page with the remaining pictures on the page. Instruct them to write words beside the pictures they describe.

Review the words labeling each pair of pictures, pointing out that they are opposite in meaning.

### Special Populations

This lesson presents several abstract tasks that will frustrate certain pupils. Young children often have difficulty distinguishing same, different, and opposite qualities. For pupils who have trouble with page 105, provide physical practice with objects that feel alike or different, smell alike or different, and taste the same or different. Make flashcards of the words you use orally *(same, different, alike, opposite)*. Do as much practice as possible with things that give pupils a physical sensation of being alike and different.

wet    dry    hard    soft    happy    sad    up    down

happy    sad
up    down
wet    dry
hard    soft

name

page 105

## Lesson 4, page 106

### Objectives
- Matches colors and shapes of objects.
- Writes a phrase that describes a pictured object by color and by name.

### Teaching

Have pupils turn to page 106 and identify the letters at the top as the lower-case letters of the alphabet. Explain that they may refer to these letters as they complete the page.

Discuss the color swatches and the color words labeling them. Explain that pupils may need to refer to the labels in order to identify and spell each color word.

Call attention to the outlines of objects and animals, identifying each label as you discuss it.

Tell pupils that the objects and animals are shown in color below. Instruct them to write a phrase describing each picture on the writing lines next to it. Point out that they will need to use a color word and the name of the object or animal itself.

If necessary, guide pupils in describing the first picture as a green lizard. Remind them that they may find the word for each color, object, or animal among the labels above. Ask pupils to refer to the letters at the top of the page if they have difficulty writing from printed words.

Emphasize neatness, correct letter formation, and spacing.

### Activity

*Letter review.* Allow individuals or groups to make letter scrapbooks. The scrapbooks might contain samples of the lower-case and capital forms of letters in pupils' best handwriting. It might also contain a page on which letters are exhibited in different typefaces cut out from a variety of magazines and newspapers. Other possibilities for pages include:

- newspaper articles with the lower-case and capital forms of letters circled throughout;
- list of classmates' names beginning with given letters;
- pictures of objects whose names begin with given letters.

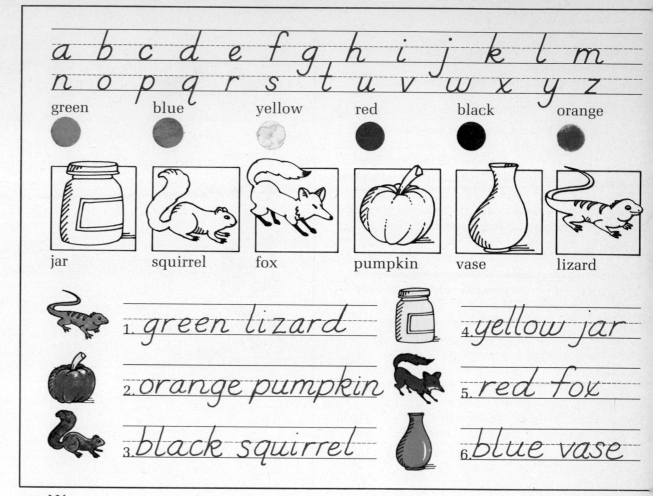

page 106

# SECTION 30

**Pages 107, 108, 109, 110**

Lesson 1, page 107
Lesson 2, page 108
Lesson 3, page 109
Lesson 4, page 110

## Lesson 1, page 107

### Objective
- Writes the letters that are shown beside each number on a telephone.

### Preparation
*Ahead of time.* If possible, provide real dial and push-botton telephones for pupils to examine. If you have access to a phone that plugs into a jack, you may simply unplug it and bring it to school. If not, you may be able to borrow some from your local telephone company.

*Class time.* Display the telephone(s). Begin the discussion by pointing out that some telephones have a dial and others have buttons to push. Identify the type(s) of telephone(s) you have on display, and demonstrate its (their) use. Point out that there are capital letters by most numbers on a telephone. Explain that letters can be part of a phone number, but that most telephone numbers consist of only numbers.

### Teaching
Have pupils turn to page 107 and study the dial and push-button types of telephones.

Ask pupils to note which letters are next to each number on the dial and push-button telephones. During the discussion, guide pupils in discovering that the same letters are beside the same numbers on each type of telephone.

Call attention to the numbers and writing lines below. Explain that pupils are to write the capital

page 107

letters that appear next to each number on the telephones. Point out that the first one has been completed for them. Ask students which capital letters appear next to the number 2 on the telephone (*A, B,* and *C*) and have pupils trace the capital letters *A, B,* and *C* on the writing line beside the number 2. Ask pupils to continue independently. Emphasize correct letter formation and provide individual assistance if necessary.

When everyone has finished, review with pupils which letters should be next to each number on a telephone. Ask pupils which letters are not used on the telephone (*Q* and *Z*).

### Activities
*Background information on telephones.* The telephone company often has some interesting leaflets for schoolchildren. You might check to see if they have some material that would be appropriate for your grade level.

139

*Emergency telephone use.* Point out that 0 is used when dialing the operator. Explain who telephone operators are and why people call them. Point out that sometimes people need to call the operator when making long-distance telephone calls. Explain that people also call an operator when there is an emergency and they need to call the police, the fire department, or the hospital quickly. If people do not have these numbers on hand near their telephones, calling the operator is the quickest way to call these places. If your area has 911 emergency dialing, include this information in the discussion.

## Lesson 2, page 108

### Objectives
• Associates an object with a place.
• Writes appropriate place name beside a picture.

### Teaching

Have pupils turn to page 108. Identify with pupils each place pictured at the top of the page. Point out that some of the places have two words in their names. Ask which one has only one word in its name (LIBRARY). If necessary, discuss the things you might get at each place.

Tell pupils to look at the pictures below. Then instruct pupils to write the name of the place each person has just come from on the appropriate writing line. Tell them to refer to the name in the picture at the top of the page for correct spelling.

If necessary, provide individual assistance by discussing each picture and asking where that person has just come from. This is the first time children will write with all capital letters when there are no D'Nealian models on the page. Give extra help where needed.

page 108

### Activity

*I am going on a trip game.* Tell pupils, "I am going on a trip to the Grocery Store, what can I find there?" Pupils should then name things that can be found in a grocery store. Follow the same procedure for the Hardware Store, Post Office, and Library. Pupils can make a list of the different things they would find in these places. Give as much help as needed with spelling.

# Lesson 3, page 109

## Objective

• Writes a sentence with correct punctuation (period, apostrophe, question mark).

## Teaching

Have pupils turn to page 109. Call attention to the punctuation marks at the top. Identify the period and have pupils write a period in the space following. Ask pupils where a period may be used. They will probably respond that a period is often used at the end of a sentence. Some students may also recall that periods are also used after a person's initial or forms of address, such as *Ms.*, *Mrs.*, and *Mr*.

Ask pupils to tell you what the next punctuation mark is and how it is used. Pupils should respond that it is an apostrophe and is often used with the letter *s* after a person's name to show that the person possesses or owns something. Have pupils write an apostrophe.

Continue with the review by asking what the last punctuation mark is and how it is used. Pupils will probably respond that it is a question mark and is used at the end of a question. Have pupils write a question mark by the model question mark.

Call attention to the picture and read the sentences. Ask pupils to identify each punctuation mark within the sentences, reviewing the reason for its use.

Ask pupils to write the sentences on the writing lines below. Emphasize correct formation of letters and punctuation marks. Remind pupils to leave the appropriate amount of space between words. Review with pupils that sentences and questions begin with a capital letter. Circulate among pupils to provide assistance with letter formation.

## Special Populations

The language concepts represented by punctuation marks are far too abstract for some pupils. Pupils who have difficulty with page 109 may also have trouble using punctuation signals in reading. These children often develop a mechanical sense of what punctuation marks mean in printed material, but they have much difficulty learning to use punctuation correctly in writing. Do not expect these pupils to grasp the abstract concepts of the period, apostrophe, and question mark in this lesson. Help them place the marks correctly as the sentences are copied, but do not press for full understanding of the reasons why.

name

. , ?

*It is dark outside.*
*Jo's bike is in the yard.*
*Can you see the bike?*

page 109

## Lesson 4, page 110

### Objective

• Chooses a word to complete a sentence.

### Preparation

*Ahead of time.* Make sure each pupil has a set of crayons.

### Teaching ■

Have pupils turn to page 110. Call attention to the box and the label *My Picture* in the upper left-hand corner. Have pupils draw and color their own picture in the box.

When pupils have finished their self-portraits, discuss the color words and number words to the right. Tell pupils that they will use some of these words to complete sentences about themselves.

Read the first incomplete sentence to pupils. Tell pupils to decide which word should be used in the sentence to describe themselves. Then have pupils write the completed sentence on the writing line below.

Continue guidance in this manner, emphasizing correct letter formation and selection of words to complete sentences. Provide help with spelling if words other than those on the page are needed.

When pupils have completed this page, refer to the last part of the lesson for page 111.

### Activity

*A Book About Me.* Pupils love to write about themselves and will use their best handwriting when making a book.

Provide white 9-inch by 12-inch construction paper with holes punched along the side. Later the books will be put together with yarn or brads.

Discuss with pupils what they would like to include in this book about themselves. When decisions have been made, have pupils label each page with a heading. Some possible headings might include: *Me, My Family, My Home, My Pets, My Favorite Food, My*

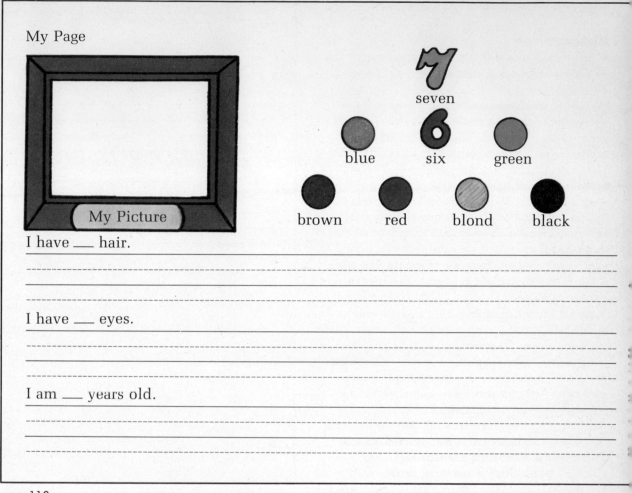

page 110

*School, My Best Friend, My Happiest Time* (or *Experience*) and on and on. After each page has been labeled, allow children time to illustrate each page. If they want to write anything else in their books, such as names of people, foods, and so on, provide assistance with spelling.

**Page 111**

**Objectives**
- Writes sample of handwriting.
- Compares samples of own handwriting on page.
- Evaluates own manuscript writing.

**Teaching** ▬▬▬▬▬

*After page 16.* Call attention to the numbers 0-10 at the top of the page. Tell pupils to write the numbers, using their best handwriting, on the line beginning with a star.

Have pupils put their fingers on the next star at the beginning of a writing line. Instruct them to use their best handwriting as they write their own names on that writing line.

*After page 54.* Ask pupils to locate the first blank writing line that has a round dot at the beginning. Explain that they are going to write, in their best handwriting, the numbers 0-10. Emphasize correct number formation, telling pupils to refer to the models at the top.

When pupils have finished writing the row of numbers, tell them to find the next round dot at the beginning of a blank writing line. Explain that they will use their best handwriting to write their names on this line. When pupils have finished, ask if they think they have improved in writing numbers and their names since the first of the year.

Direct attention to the last blank writing line that begins with a round dot. Discuss the pictures above this writing line and identify the labels. Point out the number of words in each phrase. Explain that they are to write *a big sandwich* and *a pile of junk* on the writing lines beginning with the round dot. Emphasize correct letter formation, spacing, and neatness.

*After page 110.* Have pupils put their fingers on the first square at the beginning of a blank writing line. Instruct pupils to use their best handwriting to write the numbers.

Tell pupils to locate the next writing line beginning with a square and write their own names in their best

0 1 2 3 4 5 6 7 8 9 10

★ _____

● _____

■ _____

my name

★ _____

● _____

■ _____

*a big sandwich*     *a pile of junk*

● _____

■ _____

page 111

handwriting.

Call attention to the pictures and labels near the bottom of the page. Ask pupils to use their best handwriting to write the phrases *a big sandwich* and *a pile of junk.*

When pupils have finished, have them review the three lines of numbers and evaluate their handwriting to determine if their number formation has improved during the year. Carry out the same type of evaluation with pupils' names and the phrases at the bottom of the page.

# Index